Oracle ASM 12c Pocket Reference Guide

Charles Kim

Nitin Vengurlekar

Viscosity North America Gold Partner

Exadata Experts
Private Database Cloud Experts
@ViscosityNA

DEDICATION

This Oracle ASM 12c Pocket Reference Guide is dedicated to our children:
Isaiah, Jeremiah, Noah
Ishan, Nisha

TABLE OF CONTENTS

Additional Books That We Authored

Additional books authored in 2014

ABOUT THE AUTHOR - Charles

Charles Kim is an Oracle ACE Director, Oracle Certified DBA, a Certified RAC Expert and Certified Exadata Implementation Specialist. Charles is also a VMware vExpert and a VMware Certified Professional. Charles specializes in RAC, Exadata, Virtualization and authored 7 books:
1. Oracle Database 11g New Features for DBA and Developers
2. Linux Recipes for Oracle DBAs
3. Oracle Data Guard 11g Handbook
4. Virtualizing Mission Critical Oracle Databases
5. Hadoop As A Service
6. Oracle ASM 12c Pocket Reference Guide
7. Expert Exadata Handbook

Charles holds certifications in Oracle, VMware, Red Hat Linux, and Microsoft and has over 23 years of Oracle experience on mission and business critical databases. Charles presents regularly at local, regional, national and international Oracle conferences including IOUG Collaborate, VMware World, and Oracle OpenWorld on topics of RAC, ASM, Linux Best Practices, Data Guard Best Practices, VMware virtualization, Oracle VMware virtualization, and 7×24 High Availability Considerations. Charles is the technical editor of the Automatic Storage Management book by Oracle Press and contributing author to the Database Cloud Storage: The Essential Guide to Oracle Automatic Storage Management book. Charles blogs regularly at http://blog.dbaexpert.com and http://oravm.com.

Charles is the current Vice President and Vendor Liaison of the Cloud Computing SIG for the Independent Oracle User Group. Charles blogs regularly at DBAExpert.com/blog and OraVM.com websites.
His linkedin profile is: http://www.linkedin.com/in/chkim
His twitter tag is: @racdba

ABOUT THE AUTHOR - Nitin

Nitin Vengurlekar is the co-founder and CTO of Viscosity North America, a leader in virtualization, Oracle Engineered Systems, Private Database Cloud and RAC implementations. At Viscosity Nitin is responsible for partner relationship and end-2-end solution deployment.

Prior to joining Viscosity, Nitin worked for Oracle for more than 17 years, mostly in the Real Application Cluster (RAC) engineering group, with main emphasis on ASM/storage, and RAC integration. The last three years was the spent as Database Cloud Architect/Evangelist in the Oracle's Cloud Strategy Group in charge of Private Database Cloud messaging.

Nitin is a well-known Oracle technologist and speaker in the areas of Oracle Storage, high availability, Oracle RAC, and private database cloud. He is the author of Database Cloud Storage, Oracle Automatic Storage Management and the Data Guard Handbook and has written many papers on storage, database internals, database tuning, and served as a contributor to Oracle documentation as well as Oracle education material.

With more than 25 years of IT experience, including OS390 Systems Programming, Storage Administration, System and Database Administration, Nitin is a seasoned systems architect who has successfully assisted numerous customers in deploying highly available Oracle systems.

Follow me on Twitter -> @dbcloudshifu

Introduction

When Automatic Storage Management (ASM) was introduced in 10gR1, it was simply marketed as the volume manager for the Oracle database. However, ASM has now grown into becoming an integral part of the enterprise stack.   ASM is now not only a significant part of the Oracle Clusterware stack, but is also a core component of engineered systems such as Exadata and ODA.   Oracle 12c was announced in 2012, and along with this 12c release, came significant changes for ASM.

The primary audience of this Pocket Reference Guide is aimed at database architects, database machine administrators and managers who support databases that run on ASM or Exadata.

Background

When Automatic Storage Management (ASM) was introduced in 10gR1, it was simply marketed as the volume manager for the Oracle database. ASM was designed as a purpose-built host based volume management and file system that is integrated with the Oracle database. It is built on stripping and mirroring methodology (SAME) files across as many disks as possible and providing the ability of rebalancing the file layout, online whenever the physical storage configuration changes. ASM is built on the Oracle instance architecture. From the users view, ASM exposes a small number of Disk Groups. These Disk Groups consists of ASM disks and files that are stripped across all the disks in a Disk Group. The Disk Groups are global in nature and database instances running individually or in clusters have shared access to the Disk Groups and the files within them. The ASM instances communication amongst themselves and form an ASM cluster.

These simple ideas delivered a powerful solution that eliminates many headaches DBAs and Storage Administrators once had with managing storage in an Oracle environment.

However, ASM has now grown into becoming an integral part of the enterprise stack. ASM is now not only a significant part of the Oracle Clusterware stack, but is also a core component of engineered systems such as Exadata and ODA. Oracle 12c was announced in 2013, and along with this 12c release, came significant changes for ASM. This paper will cover some of key management and high availability features introduced in 12c ASM. Readers will get a glimpse of these advancements, the history behind the new features, and why these features are a necessary part of the future of ASM.

The main theme of 12c ASM is extreme scalability, management of real-world data types and removes many of the limitations of previous ASM generation. This paper we will preview some of the key features of ASM and Cloud Storage in Oracle 12c. Note, that this book will provide an overview of the new key features and optimizations in particular in the areas of:

- Better HA & Business Continuity
- Better agility and flexibility
- Better performance and scalability

1 Automatic Storage Management

ASM Specific Initialization Parameters

At a minimum, you should see the following initialization parameters for the ASM instance:

```
*.cluster_database= true   #-- If RAC
*.asm_diskstring = '/dev/emcpower*'
*.instance_type=asm
*.processes=300
*.asm_diskgroups = 'DATA','FRA'
*.memory_target=1300M
```

NOTES:

1. Starting in Oracle Database 11g Release 2, instead of setting the shared_pool_size and db_cache_size parameters, best practice is to set MEMORY_TARGET parameter to 1.3 - 1.5 GB and be done. Determining to leverage hugepages is a consideration by setting SGA_TARGET instead.

2. We no longer need to set the ASM_DISKGROUPS parameter. This parameter will be automatically be populated when you create database related disk groups. For non-database specific disk groups such as ACFS disk group for GoldenGate shared file system, you will need to update this parameter manually:

```
SQL>  ALTER SYSTEM set ASM_DISKGROUPS='DATA','FRA','GG' SID='*'
SCOPE=both;
```

ASM Diskgroups

Create diskgroup - External Redundancy (SQL Method)

```
create diskgroup DATA01 external redundancy
disk 'ORCL:DATA01_DISK1',
'ORCL:DATA01_DISK2',
'ORCL:DATA01_DISK3',
'ORCL:DATA01_DISK4'
ATTRIBUTE
'au_size' = '4M',
'compatible.rdbms' = '11.2.0.3',
'compatible.asm' = '11.2.0.3',
'compatible.advm' = '11.2.0.3';
```

External Redundancy (XML Method)

```
data01.xml

<dg name="DATA01" redundancy="external">
<dsk string="ORCL:DATA01_DISK1" />
<dsk string="ORCL:DATA01_DISK2" />
<dsk string="ORCL:DATA01_DISK3" />
<dsk string="ORCL:DATA01_DISK4" />
<a name="compatible.asm" value="11.2.0.3"/>
<a name="compatible.rdbms" value="11.2.0.3"/>
<a name="compatible.advm" value="11.2.0.3"/>
<a name="au_size" value="4M"/> </dg>

$ asmcmd mkdg data01.xml
```

Normal Redundancy (SQL Method)

```
CREATE DISKGROUP disk_group_1
NORMAL REDUNDANCY
FAILGROUP
failure_group_1
DISK
'/dev/diska1' NAME diska1,
'/dev/diska2' NAME diska2,
FAILGROUP failure_group_2
DISK
'/dev/diskb1' NAME diskb1,
'/dev/diskb2' NAME diskb2;
```

List Disk Groups and Information

```
ASMCMD> lsdg data
```

```
ASMCMD> lsdg data
State    Type    Rebal  Sector  Block       AU  Total_MB  Free_MB  Req_mir_free_MB  Usable_file_MB  Offline_disks  Voting_files  Name
MOUNTED  EXTERN  N      512     4096  4194304    63996    41984                0           41984              0             N  DATA/
```

List ASM Disks

```
ASMCMD> lsdsk -t -G DATA
Create_Date  Mount_Date  Repair_Timer  Path
22-APR-14    05-AUG-14   0             ORCL:DATA1
22-APR-14    05-AUG-14   0             ORCL:DATA2
```

Add Disks

```
ALTER DISKGROUP DATA
ADD DISK 'ORCL:DATA05'
rebalance power 11 wait;
```

NOTES:

With compatible.asm=11.2.0.3+, you are not limited to power 11

Mount and Unmount Disk Groups

```
SQL> alter diskgroup DATA mount;
SQL> alter diskgroup DATA dismount;
Or
asmcmd> mount DATA
asmcmd> umount DATA
```

Drop Disk Group

```
SQL> DROP DISKGROUP DATA INCLUDING CONTENTS;
or
ASMCMD> dropdg -r -f data
```

Drop a Disk From a Disk Group

```
alter diskgroup data drop disk
'DATA_0001',
'DATA_0002'
rebalance power 11 wait;
```

Undrop Disks Clause of the Alter Disk Group

```
ALTER DISKGROUP DATA UNDROP DISKS;
```

Rebalance Disk Group

```
SQL> ALTER DISKGROUP DATA REBALANCE POWER 5;
SQL> SELECT * FROM V$ASM_OPERATION;
or
ASMCMD> rebal --power 5 DATA
ASMCMD> lsop
```

Check Disk Group

```
SQL> alter diskgroup data check;
SQL> alter diskgroup data check norepair;
or
ASMCMD> chkdg --repair
ASMCMD> chkdg
```

Clone non-RAC (Non-Clustered) Grid Infrastructure Home - 11.2 +

```
export ORACLE_HOME=/apps/oracle/product/11.2.0/grid
sudo chmod 770 $ORACLE_HOME

cd $ORACLE_HOME/clone/bin
$ORACLE_HOME/perl/bin/perl clone.pl ORACLE_BASE="/apps/oracle"
ORACLE_HOME="/apps/oracle/product/11.2.0/grid" OSDBA_GROUP=oinstall
OSOPER_GROUP=oinstall ORACLE_HOME_NAME=Ora11g_gridinfrahome1
INVENTORY_LOCATION=/apps/oraInventory

# /apps/oraInventory/orainstRoot.sh
# /apps/oracle/product/11.2.0/grid/root.sh
# /apps/oracle/product/11.2.0/grid/perl/bin/perl -
I/apps/oracle/product/11.2.0/grid/perl/lib -
I/apps/oracle/product/11.2.0/grid/crs/install
/apps/oracle/product/11.2.0/grid/crs/install/roothas.pl

$ sudo chmod 750 $ORACLE_HOME
$ crsctl stop has
$ srvctl add listener
$ srvctl add asm -d 'ORCL:*'
$ srvctl start listener
$ srvctl start asm
```

ASM DICTIONARY VIEWS

v$asm_alias	Lists all aliases in all currently mounted diskgroups
v$asm_client	Lists all the databases currently

	accessing the diskgroups
v$asm_disk	Lists all the disks discovered by the ASM instance
v$asm_diskgroup	Lists all the diskgroups discovered by the ASM instance
v$asm_file	Lists all files that belong to diskgroups mounted by the ASM instance
v$asm_operation	Reports information about current active operations. Rebalance activity is reported in this view
v$asm_template	Lists all the templates currently mounted by the ASM instance
v$asm_diskgroup_stat	Same as v$asm_diskgroup but does not discover new diskgroups. Use this view instead of v$asm_diskgroup
v$asm_disk_stat	Same as v$asm_disk but does not discover new disks. Use this view instead of v$asm_disk

Relevant srvctl commands

Add	`srvctl add asm -n rac3 -i +ASM3 -o /u01/app/oracle/product/11.2.0.4/asm`
Enable ASM	`srvctl enable asm -n rac3 -i +ASM3`
Set Spfile	`srvctl modify asm -p +DATA/<full-filepath>`
Disable ASM	`srvctl disable asm -n rac3 -i +ASM3`
Start ASM	`srvctl start asm -n rac3`
Stop ASM	`srvctl stop asm -n rac3`
Config	`srvctl config asm -n rac1`
Remove ASM	`srvctl remove asm -n rac1`

Status ASM	`srvctl status asm` `srvctl status asm -n rac1`
Modify	`srvctl modify asm -o -n rac1`
Status DG	`srvctl status diskgroup -g data`
Remove DG	`srvctl remove diskgroup -g` `<current_dg>`
Enable/Disable DG	`srvctl enable diskgroup -g DATA` `srvctl disable diskgroup -g DATA`
Start DG	`srvctl start diskgroup -g DATA`
Stop DG	`srvctl stop diskgroup -g DATA`

Rename Disk Group

```
$ srvctl stop diskgroup -g DATA
$ crsctl stat res -t
$ renamedg phase=both dgname=DATA newdgname=DATA_EMC verbose=true
```

Prepare block devices for ASM

On Intel-based systems such as Linux/Windows, the first 63 blocks have been reserved for the master boot record (MBR). Therefore, the first data partition starts with offset at 31.5KB (that is, 63 times 512 bytes equals 31.5KB).

This offset can cause misalignment on many storage arrays' memory cache or RAID configurations, causing performance degradation due to overlapping I/Os. This performance impact is especially evident for large block I/O workloads, such as parallel query processing and full table scans.

The following shows how to manually perform the alignment using sfdisk or the parted command against an EMC Powerpath device. Note that this procedure is applicable to any OS device that needs to partitioned aligned.

Partition Alignment with sfdisk (Has limitation with < 2TB)

```
# -- Partition alignment of OCR / Vote Disks with 1MB offset
echo "2048,," | sfdisk -uS /dev/emcpowera
echo "2048,," | sfdisk -uS /dev/emcpowerb
echo "2048,," | sfdisk -uS /dev/emcpowerc

# -- Partition alignment of Data / FRA disks with 4MB offset
echo "8192,," | sfdisk -uS /dev/emcpowerd
echo "8192,," | sfdisk -uS /dev/emcpowere
echo "8192,," | sfdisk -uS /dev/emcpowerf
echo "8192,," | sfdisk -uS /dev/emcpowerg
echo "8192,," | sfdisk -uS /dev/emcpowerh
```

Here's a sample output:

```
Checking that no-one is using this disk right now ...
OK
Disk /dev/emcpowerb: 1018 cylinders, 166 heads, 62 sectors/track
Old situation:
No partitions found
New situation:
Units = sectors of 512 bytes, counting from 0
   Device Boot    Start      End    #sectors  Id  System
/dev/emcpowerb1            2048  10477255   10475208  83  Linux
/dev/emcpowerb2               0        -          0   0  Empty
/dev/emcpowerb3               0        -          0   0  Empty
```

```
/dev/emcpowerb4            0         -         0    0  Empty
Warning: no primary partition is marked bootable (active)
This does not matter for LILO, but the DOS MBR will not boot this disk.
Successfully wrote the new partition table
Re-reading the partition table ...
```

Check that partitions exist

```
# /sbin/fdisk -l /dev/emcpowerb

Disk /dev/emcpowerb: 5368 MB, 5368709120 bytes
166 heads, 62 sectors/track, 1018 cylinders
Units = cylinders of 10292 * 512 = 5269504 bytes

         Device Boot      Start         End      Blocks   Id  System
/dev/emcpowerb1               1        1018     5237604   83  Linux
```

Partition Alignment with parted command

```
for DISK in a b c d e f g h
do
   /sbin/parted -s emcpower${DISK} mkpart primary ext4 2048s 100%
done
```

View Partition Alignment

```
sudo /sbin/parted emcpower${DISK} print
```

Erase ASM disk to clear and prepare block devices

```
dd if=/dev/zero of=/dev/emcpowera1 bs=1M count=100
```

NOTES:

Exercise extreme caution as it will destroy all the data on the disk

Read ASM Disk Header

```
dd if=/dev/emcpowera1 bs=512 count=1 |od -a

1+0 records in
1+0 records out
512 bytes (512 B) copied, 5.2776e-05 s, 9.7 MB/s
0000000 soh stx soh soh nul nul nul nul nul nul nul nul   a   @ etx   ]
0000020 nul nul nul nul nul nul nul nul nul nul nul nul nul nul nul nul
0000040   O   R   C   L   D   I   S   K   R   E   C   O   1 nul nul nul
0000060 nul nul nul nul nul nul nul nul nul nul nul nul nul nul nul nul
0000100 nul nul dle  ff nul nul soh etx   R   E   C   O   1 nul nul nul
0000120 nul nul nul nul nul nul nul nul nul nul nul nul nul nul nul nul
0000140 nul nul nul nul nul nul nul nul   R   E   C   O nul nul nul nul
0000160 nul nul nul nul nul nul nul nul nul nul nul nul nul nul nul nul
```

```
0000200 nul nul nul nul nul nul nul nul   R   E   C   O   l nul nul nul
0000220 nul nul nul nul nul nul nul nul nul nul nul nul nul nul nul nul
*
0000300 nul nul nul nul nul nul nul nul   J dc2   w soh nul   X   I   ,
0000320   .  sp   w soh nul   \   -   O nul stx nul dle nul nul   @ nul
0000340 nul   n ack nul del   l nul nul etx nul nul nul soh nul nul nul
0000360 stx nul nul nul  nl nul nul nul nul nul nul nul nul nul nul nul
0000400 nul nul dle  nl   J dc2   w soh nul  sp   F   , nul nul nul nul
0000420 nul nul nul nul nul nul nul nul nul nul nul nul soh nul nul nul
0000440 nul nul nul nul nul nul nul nul nul nul nul nul nul nul nul nul
*
0001000
```

ASMLIB Installation

RHEL 6.4 and higher

For ASMLIB, we have three RPM packages that need to be installed:

1. kmod-oracleasm
2. oracleasmlib
3. oracleasm-support

https://access.redhat.com/site/solutions/315643

For RedHat Linux customers (RHEL 6.4 and higher), kmod-oracleasm is only available from the Red Hat Network (RHN) and can be installed from the RHEL Server Supplementary (v. 6 64-bit x86_64) channel. oracleasmlib and oracleasm-support packages are available for download from Oracle at http://www.oracle.com/technetwork/server-storage/linux/asmlib/rhel6-1940776.html.

Here's what the installation steps look like in RHEL 6.4 and higher. It does not look any different than before except we are playing with a new player kmod-oracleasm from Red Hat instead of Oracle:

```
# ls -l *oracleasm*
-rw-r--r-- 1 root root 35044 Aug 22 20:41 kmod-oracleasm-2.0.6.rh1-2.el6.x86_64.rpm
-rw-r--r-- 1 root root 13300 Aug 22 20:45 oracleasmlib-2.0.4-1.el6.x86_64.rpm
-rw-r--r-- 1 root root 74984 Aug 22 20:56 oracleasm-support-2.1.8-1.el6.x86_64.rpm
```

Installation is done with a simple rpm -ihv command on each of the RPMs that we downloaded. There does not seem to be any dependencies between any of the RPMs. In this example, we will install the kmod-oracleasm RPM, followed by oracleasmlib, followed by oracle-support RPMs.

```
# rpm -ihv kmod-oracleasm-2.0.6.rh1-2.el6.x86_64.rpm
warning: kmod-oracleasm-2.0.6.rh1-2.el6.x86_64.rpm: Header V3 RSA/SHA256 Signature, key
ID fd431d51: NOKEY
Preparing...                ########################################### [100%]
```

```
   1:kmod-oracleasm            ######################################### [100%]


# rpm -ihv oracleasmlib-2.0.4-1.el6.x86_64.rpm
warning: oracleasmlib-2.0.4-1.el6.x86_64.rpm: Header V3 RSA/SHA256 Signature, key ID
ec551f03: NOKEY
Preparing...                    ######################################### [100%]
   1:oracleasmlib               ######################################### [100%]

# rpm -ihv oracleasm-support-2.1.8-1.el6.x86_64.rpm
warning: oracleasm-support-2.1.8-1.el6.x86_64.rpm: Header V3 RSA/SHA256 Signature, key ID
ec551f03: NOKEY
Preparing...                    ######################################### [100%]
   1:oracleasm-support          ######################################### [100%]
```

Oracle Linux Customers

We are assuming that you have already installed kmod-oracleasm and oracleasm-support RPMs with yum:

```
# yum install kmod-oracleasm -y
# yum install oracleasm-support -y
```

For Oracle Linux customers, oracleasmlib is not available from the default yum repository. You can pull the oracleasmlib RPM from http://www.oracle.com/technetwork/server-storage/linux/asmlib/ol6-1709075.html

ASMLIB Configuration (Same for Red Hat and Oracle Linux)

After we install the RPMs, we need to configure ASMLIB to scan immediately and to re-start on reboot for the Oracle user.

```
# service oracleasm configure
Configuring the Oracle ASM library driver.

This will configure the on-boot properties of the Oracle ASM library
driver.  The following questions will determine whether the driver is
loaded on boot and what permissions it will have.  The current values
will be shown in brackets ('[]').  Hitting <ENTER> without typing an
answer will keep that current value.  Ctrl-C will abort.

Default user to own the driver interface []: oracle
Default group to own the driver interface []: dba
```

```
Start Oracle ASM library driver on boot (y/n) [n]: y
Scan for Oracle ASM disks on boot (y/n) [y]:
Writing Oracle ASM library driver configuration: done
Initializing the Oracle ASMLib driver: [  OK  ]
Scanning the system for Oracle ASMLib disks: [  OK  ]

[root@rh64a ~]# oracleasm configure
ORACLEASM_ENABLED=true
ORACLEASM_UID=oracle
ORACLEASM_GID=dba
ORACLEASM_SCANBOOT=true
ORACLEASM_SCANORDER=""
ORACLEASM_SCANEXCLUDE=""
ORACLEASM_USE_LOGICAL_BLOCK_SIZE="false"
```

As the final step in the process, we need to initialize ASMLIB and confirm
that it was successfully started:

```
# oracleasm init
Creating /dev/oracleasm mount point: /dev/oracleasm
Loading module "oracleasm": oracleasm
Configuring "oracleasm" to use device physical block size
Mounting ASMlib driver filesystem: /dev/oracleasm

# oracleasm status
Checking if ASM is loaded: yes
Checking if /dev/oracleasm is mounted: yes
```

ASMLIB Commands - Most as root

```
oracleasm start
oracleasm stop
oracleasm restart
oracleasm configure -i

oracleasm status
oracleasm enable
oracleasm disable
oracleasm deletedisk

oracleasm createdisk DATA_DISK1 /dev/mapper/data_disk1p1

oracleasm querydisk /dev/emcpowerb1
oracleasm querydisk DATA_DISK1

oracleasm renamedisk /dev/sdb1 VOL1
oracleasm force-renamedisk DATA_DISK1 NEW_DATA_DISK1
```

```
oracleasm scandisks
oracleasm listdisks
```

Multi-Path Configuration with ASMLIB

Modify /etc/sysconfig/oracleasm (on each node) as root:

```
# ORACLEASM_SCANORDER: Matching patterns to order disk scanning
ORACLEASM_SCANORDER="dm-" # For Device Mapper
# ORACLEASM_SCANORDER="emcpower" # For EMC Powerpath
# ORACLEASM_SCANEXCLUDE: Matching patterns to exclude disks from scan
ORACLEASM_SCANEXCLUDE="sd"
```

Volume Management

Create	volcreate -G DBA_PD101 -s 32g dba_vol
Resize	volresize -G DBA_PD101 -s 64g dba_vol
Enable	volenable -G DBA_PD101 -a
Disable	voldisable -G DBA_PD101 dba_vol voldisable -G DBA_PD101 -a
Set Attributes	volset -G DBA_PD101 --usagestring 'No files' dba_vol
Info	volinfo -G DATA01 vol_dba
Delete	voldelete -G DBA_PD101 dba_vol

SQL Method

```
SQL> alter diskgroup data add volume vol_dba size 12g;
SQL> alter diskgroup data resize volume vol_dba size 16g;
SQL> alter diskgroup data disable volume vol_dba;
SQL> alter diskgroup data enable volume vol_dba;
SQL> alter diskgroup all disable volume all;
```

Fundamentals of asmcmd

The asmcmd command line interface is similar to the korn shell or bourne shell. Lot of the commands that are available in the Unix shell is available in the asmcmd command line interface. All though not complete in terms of providing a shell access, asmcmd does provide a substantial amount of interaction to the ASM file system. As a system administrator or as a DBA, you want to maximize the usage of the asmcmd shell. This section will focus on the key feature sets available in the asmcmd command line interface.

Important ASMCMD Commands

cd	Changes the current directory to the specified directory
du	Displays the total disk space occupied by ASM files in the specified ASM directory and all its subdirectories, recursively
find	Lists the paths of all occurrences of the specified name (with wildcards) under the specified directory
ls +data/testdb	Lists the contents of an ASM directory, the attributes of the specified file, or the names and attributes of all disk groups
lsct	Lists information about current ASM clients
lsdg	Lists all disk groups and their attributes
lsdsk -k	To see V$ASM_DISK information in preformatted columns without having to write SQL statement
mkalias	Creates an alias for a system-generated filename
mkdir	Creates ASM directories
pwd	Displays the path of the current ASM directory
rm	Deletes the specified ASM files or directories

rm -f	
rmalias	Deletes the specified alias, retaining the file that the alias points to
lsdsk	Lists disks visible to ASM
md_backup	Creates a backup of all of the mounted disk groups
md_restore	Restores disk groups from a backup
mkalias	Creates an alias for system-generated filenames
remap	Repairs a range of physical blocks on a disk
cp	Copies files into and out of ASM: • ASM diskgroup to OS file system • OS file system to ASM diskgroup • ASM diskgroup to another ASM diskgroup on the same server • ASM disk group to ASM diskgroup on a remote server
lsop	Displays one row for every active long-running operation executing in the ASM instance from V$ASM_OPERATION

Commands relative to SPFILE

spget	Retrieves the location of the Oracle ASM SPFILE
	`ASMCMD> spget`
	`+OCR/vnarac12a/ASMPARAMETERFILE/registry.253.84193`
	`7097`

spcopy	Copies an Oracle ASM SPFILE from source to destination
	`ASMCMD> spcopy`
	`+OCR/vnarac12a/ASMPARAMETERFILE/registry.253.84193`
	`7097 /tmp/spfile+ASM`

spmove	Moves an Oracle ASM SPFILE from source to

	destination and along the way updates the GPnP profile

spbackup	Backs up the ASM spfile
	`ASMCMD> spbackup`
	`+OCR/vnarac12a/ASMPARAMETERFILE/registry.253.84193`
	`7097 /tmp/spfile+ASMBackup`

spset	Sets the new location of the ASM SPFILE `ASMCMD> spset +DATA/asm/ASMspfile.ora`

dsget	Gets the current ASM diskstring value
	`ASMCMD> dsget`
	`profile: /dev/mapper/mpath*`
	`parameter: /dev/mapper/mpath*`

dsget (from GPnP profile)	Gets the current ASM diskstring value
	`ASMCMD> dsget --profile`
	`profile: /dev/mapper/mpath*`

dsset	Sets the current ASM diskstring value `ASMCMD> dsget ORCL:*`

Connecting to asmcmd

To access the asmcmd shell in interactive mode, you must satisfy two requirements. First, your ORACLE_SID must point to a valid ASM instance such as +ASM or +ASM# for RAC implementations. Second, your ORACLE_HOME must point an ORACLE_HOME that houses the asmcmd executable in the $ORACLE_HOME/bin directory. In all the Unix and Linux systems, you should be able to source the oraenv file from /usr/local/bin directory and enter either +ASM or +ASM# (where # is the instance number for ASM). To connect to the asmcmd command line interface, you simply type asmcmd from the operating system.

> Tip: asmcmd has one special parameter, the –p parameter, which is equivalent to the PS1 environment variable in Linux.

The oraenv file looks at the +ASM instance listed in the /etc/oratab file that looks something like this:

`+ASM:/apps/oracle/product/12.1.0/ASM:Y`

You can source the oraenv file and change your environment to the

+ASM instance as shown here:

```
DBATOOLS > . oraenv
ORACLE_SID = [PROD] ? +ASM
```

Your Linux/Unix environment variables point to the +ASM instance. To connect to the ASM instance using the asmcmd shell, pass the –p option:

```
+ASM > asmcmd -p
ASMCMD [+] >
```

Tip: Create a Unix/Linux alias in the .bashrc or .aliases file for asmcmd='asmcmd –p'.

Linux / Unix Like Commands

rm

The rm command in asmcmd is similar to the rm command in the Unix operating system. Here's a rm example to delete all the files associated with the DBADEV database:

```
ASMCMD> cd +data
ASMCMD> rm -rf PROD

ASMCMD> cd +fra
ASMCMD> rm -rf PROD
```

The rm command also accepts wildcards to delete files or directories. In the next example, you will see in action the rm command prompting a response from the administrator while deleting a file with a wildcard:

```
ASMCMD [+data/prod/datafile] > ls
TOOLS.270.655646559
docs_d_01.dbf

ASMCMD [+data/prod/datafile] > rm docs*
You may delete multiple files and/or directories.
Are you sure? (y/n) y
```

Note: The rm command is particular important when you run out of space in the archivelog destination. You can cd to the archivelog destination and remove old or backed up archivelogs from the ASM instance.

ls

The most basic commands in the asmcmd command line interface are cd and ls. These commands are very similar to their respective counterparts in the Unix world. The cd command in the asmcmd command line interface is not case sensitive and can take wildcards.

> Note: The command "cd +" in asmcmd command line interface is equivalent to the "cd /" command in Unix.

The ls command can accept numerous parameters. The standard parameters that you are accustomed to seeing in the Unix world such as the ls –l (long list), ls –lt (long list sort by timestamp), ls -ltr (long list in reverse sort order based on timestamp), and ls –ld (long listing of just directory name) are all available in the asmcmd command line interface. The ls command lacks the feature to display time stamps or the type of file with the long list parameter.

> Tip: The command "ls +" lists all the diskgroups in the ASM instance.

du

The du command displays the disk usage information for a specified directory. For example, if you want to know how much space is consumed for the DBATOOLS database in the +DATA diskgroup, you can view that information like this:

```
ASMCMD [+] > du +data/dbatools
Used_MB       Mirror_used_MB
   102                  102
```

You can specify the full path of the subdirectory with the du command to determine the sizes of the tempfile(s) for a database or the size of all the datafiles for a database or the size of the controlfile(s) for a database. In the examples below, the du command checks size of the tempfiles, datafiles and controlfile in the +DATA diskgroup:

```
ASMCMD [+data/dbadev] > du +data/dbadev/tempfile
Used_MB       Mirror_used_MB
  4002                 4002

ASMCMD [+data/dbadev] > du +data/dbadev/datafile
Used_MB       Mirror_used_MB
  6312                 6312

ASMCMD [+data/dbadev] > du +data/dbadev/controlfile
Used_MB       Mirror_used_MB
   24                   24
```

find

The find command is a powerful utility in the Unix arena and is also a powerful command in the asmcmd command line interface. The find command in the asmcmd command line interface does not have all the options that you will find in Unix. The find command has the following parameters:

```
find [-t <type>] <dir> <pattern>
```

The −t option specifies the type of file and is queried from the TYPE column in the V$ASM_FILE view. You can also specify the starting directory for the find command to search from. The last option is the pattern for the find command to match on. You can use either the percent sign(%) or the asterick(*) as wildcard characters. Let's take a look at the find command to locate all the files in the data diskgroup that have the filenames SYS somewhere in the filename:

```
ASMCMD [+] > find -t datafile +data *sys*
+data/DBADEV/DATAFILE/SYSAUX.257.655588275
+data/DBADEV/DATAFILE/SYSTEM.258.655588211
```

If you want to locate all the online redo logs in the +DATA diskgroups, you can use the –t option and specify onlinelog as the parameter with the * wildcard for the pattern as shown here:

```
ASMCMD [+] > find -t onlinelog +data *
+data/DBADEV/ONLINELOG/group_1.264.655587995
+data/DBADEV/ONLINELOG/group_2.263.655588025
+data/DBADEV/ONLINELOG/group_3.262.655588055
+data/DBADEV/ONLINELOG/group_4.261.655588099
+data/DBADEV/ONLINELOG/group_5.260.655588129
+data/DBADEV/ONLINELOG/group_6.259.655588177
```

You can use the find command to locate all the files associated with a database for a given diskgroup. You can specify a subdirectory to the find command with a wildcard for the pattern as you can see here:

```
find +data/DBADEV %
```

lsdsk

The lsdsk command lists all the visible disks and accepts numerous parameters. If you type lsdsk without any parameters, the output will display all the disks in the ASM instance. Here's the output of the lsdsk command without any parameters:

```
ASMCMD [+] > lsdsk
Path
ORCL:DATA1
ORCL:DATA2
ORCL:DATA3
ORCL:DATA4
ORCL:FRA1
ORCL:FRA2
ORCL:FRA3
ORCL:FRA4
```

In the next example, you can specify a –d option to limit the output to a specific diskgroup:

```
ASMCMD [+] > lsdsk -d data
Path
ORCL:DATA1
ORCL:DATA2
ORCL:DATA3
ORCL:DATA4
```

The –k option displays the TOTAL_MB, NAME, FAILGROUP, PATH column information from the V$ASM_DISK view in the output.

```
ASMCMD [+] > lsdsk -k
Total_MB  Free_MB  OS_MB  Name   Failgroup  Library
Label  UDID  Product  Redund   Path
   15264    12180  15264  DATA1  DATA1      ASM Library - Generic Linux,
version 2.0.2 (KABI_V2)  DATA1             UNKNOWN  ORCL:DATA1
   15264    12184  15264  DATA2  DATA2      ASM Library - Generic Linux,
version 2.0.2 (KABI_V2)  DATA2             UNKNOWN  ORCL:DATA2
   15264    12184  15264  DATA3  DATA3      ASM Library - Generic Linux,
version 2.0.2 (KABI_V2)  DATA3             UNKNOWN  ORCL:DATA3
   15264    12181  15264  DATA4  DATA4      ASM Library - Generic Linux,
version 2.0.2 (KABI_V2)  DATA4             UNKNOWN  ORCL:DATA4
   15264    14791  15264  FRA1   FRA1       ASM Library - Generic Linux,
version 2.0.2 (KABI_V2)  FRA1              UNKNOWN  ORCL:FRA1
   15264    14795  15264  FRA2   FRA2       ASM Library - Generic Linux,
version 2.0.2 (KABI_V2)  FRA2              UNKNOWN  ORCL:FRA2
   15264    14790  15264  FRA3   FRA3       ASM Library - Generic Linux,
version 2.0.2 (KABI_V2)  FRA3              UNKNOWN  ORCL:FRA3
   15264    14793  15264  FRA4   FRA4       ASM Library - Generic Linux,
version 2.0.2 (KABI_V2)  FRA4              UNKNOWN  ORCL:FRA4
```

The –t option provides important information in terms of when the disk was added to the diskgroup, when it was mounted, how long the repair timer is and the path of the disk. Here's an output of the lsdsk command with the –t option:

```
ASMCMD [+] > lsdsk -t
Create_Date  Mount_Date  Repair_Timer  Path
24-MAY-08    25-MAY-08   0             ORCL:DATA1
24-MAY-08    25-MAY-08   0             ORCL:DATA2
24-MAY-08    25-MAY-08   0             ORCL:DATA3
24-MAY-08    25-MAY-08   0             ORCL:DATA4
24-MAY-08    25-MAY-08   0             ORCL:FRA1
24-MAY-08    25-MAY-08   0             ORCL:FRA2
24-MAY-08    25-MAY-08   0             ORCL:FRA3
24-MAY-08    25-MAY-08   0             ORCL:FRA4
```

You can take advantage of the –s option to view statistical information about each of the disks. You can view read time, write time, bytes read and bytes written to at the disk level. You can correlate the output from the –s option to find busy disks. Here's an output of the lsdsk command with the –s option:

```
ASMCMD [+] > lsdsk -s
Reads   Write  Read_Errs  Write_Errs  Read_time  Write_Time  Bytes_Read
Bytes_Written  Path
2790    1622          0           0     14.507       5.644    27713536
ORCL:DATA1
2614     754          0           0     13.302       5.912    30078976
ORCL:DATA2
3959    1694          0           0     10.938       8.385    51269632
ORCL:DATA3
4539     869          0           0     12.748       6.782    64300544
ORCL:DATA4
700     1015          0           0       .696       2.312     2864128
ORCL:FRA1
688      347          0           0       .636       2.361     2814464
ORCL:FRA2
702      336          0           0       .819       4.097     2871808
ORCL:FRA3
692      263          0           0       .767       2.135     2823680
ORCL:FRA4
```

Starting / shutting down ASM with asmcmd

```
ASMCMD [+] > shutdown
ASMCMD [+] > shutdown --immediate
ASMCMD [+] > shutdown --abort
ASMCMD [+] > startup --nomount --pfile initASM.ora
ASMCMD [+] > startup --mount
```

Tip: You should ALWAYs dismount all file systems mounted on Oracle ASM Dynamic Volume Manager (Oracle ADVM) volumes before shutting the Oracle ASM instance with the --abort option.

Copying Files In and Out of ASM

Copy File from ASM to File System

ASMCMD [+] > cp +DATA_EXAD/prod/spfileprod.ora /tmp/spfilebkup.ora

Copy File from ASM to ASM

ASMCMD> cp +data/CDB1B/spfileCDB1B.ora +RECO/CDB1B/spfileCDB1B.ora

Copy File from File System to ASM

ASMCMD [+] > cp /u01/app/oracle/product/12.1.0/dbhome_1/dbs/spfileORAPROD.ora
+DATA_EXAD/prod/spfileORAPROD.ora

Certified Expert

Connecting with SYSASM Role (Starting in Oracle Database 11g)

```
SQL> grant sysasm to sys; -- sysdba deprecated
sqlplus / as sysasm
```

ASM Rolling Upgrades

Start	alter system start rolling migration to 11.2.0.2;
Disable	alter system stop rolling migration;

Database Interactions with ASM

Database Initialization Parameters for ASM

```
*.control_files='+DATA/visk/controlfile/control1.ctl','+FRA/visk/controlfile/
control2.ctl'
*.db_create_file_dest='+DATA'
*.db_create_online_log_dest_1='+DATA'
*.db_recovery_file_dest='+DATA'
*.log_archive_dest_1='LOCATION=+DATA'
*.log_file_name_convert='+DATA/VISKDR','+DATA/VISK'  ## added for DG
```

Create Tablespace

```
create tablespace indx datafile '+data' size 32000m;
```

Add a Datafile to a Tablespace

```
alter tablespace indx add datafile '+DATA' size 32000m;
```

Migrate to ASM using RMAN

```
run
{
allocate channel d1 type disk;
backup as copy database format '+DATA';
switch database to copy;
release channel d1;
}
```

Restore Controlfile (RMAN)

```
restore controlfile to '+data01/DBATOOLS/controlfile/control01.ctl' from
'/u21/oradata/DBATOOLS/control01.ctl';
```

Restore Database to ASM using SET NEWNAME

```
run
{
allocate channel d1 type disk;
# For each datafile
set newname for datafile 1 to '+DATA';
set newname for datafile 2 to '+DATA';
restore database;
switch datafile all;
release channel d1;
}
```

Add Redo Groups

```
alter database add logfile thread 2
group 21 ('+data01','+fra01') size 1000m;
```

Create Database in ASM with dbca (Silent Mode)

```
dbca -silent \
-createDatabase \
-templateName db_gold_01.dbc \
-gdbName racdb \
-sid racdb \
-SysPassword oracle123 \
-SystemPassword oracle123 \
-emConfiguration NONE \
-redoLogFileSize 500 \
-recoveryAreaDestination FRA \
-storageType ASM \
-asmSysPassword oracle123 \
-diskGroupName DATA \
-listeners LISTENER_RAC \
-characterSet AL32UTF8 \
-nationalCharacterSet AL16UTF16 \
-databaseType MULTIPURPOSE \
-nodelist rac1,rac2,rac3 \
-initparams audit_file_dest='/oraacfs/trace/racdb/adump' \
-initparams compatible='11.2.0.3' \
-initparams db_create_file_dest='+DATA' \
-initparams db_create_online_log_dest_1='+DATA' \
-initparams db_create_online_log_dest_2='+FRA' \
-initparams diagnostic_dest='/oraacfs' \
-initparams parallel_max_servers=32 \
-initparams pga_aggregate_target=524288000 \
-initparams processes=400 \
-initparams sga_target=4294967296 \
-initparams db_recovery_file_dest='+FRA' \
-initparams db_recovery_file_dest_size=2097152000
```

IOSTAT

```
ASMCMD> iostat -G DATA
```

Group_Name	Dsk_Name	Reads	Writes
DATA	DATA1	654505505280	18783542272
DATA	DATA2	2701731549696	277859352576

Display information in IOs not bytes

```
ASMCMD> iostat --io -G DATA
```

```
Group_Name  Dsk_Name  Reads      Writes
DATA        DATA1     11387760   1460064
DATA        DATA2     127260082  15528175
```

Display information in IOs not bytes with interval

```
ASMCMD> iostat --io -G DATA 5
```

List Attributes for Disk Group

```
ASMCMD> lsattr -l -G data
```

```
Name                      Value
access_control.enabled    FALSE
access_control.umask      066
au_size                   4194304
cell.smart_scan_capable   FALSE
compatible.asm            12.1.0.0.0
compatible.rdbms          10.1.0.0.0
content.check             FALSE
content.type              data
disk_repair_time          3.6h
failgroup_repair_time     24.0h
idp.boundary              auto
idp.type                  dynamic
phys_meta_replicated      true
sector_size               512
thin_provisioned          FALSE
```

OCR and Vote Disk Restore

```
# cd $GI_HOME
# ./crsctl start crs -excl -nocrs

SQL> create diskgroup OV
normal redundancy
disk
'ORCL:PV101_DISK1', 'ORCL:PV101_DISK2',
'ORCL:PV101_DISK3'
attribute = '11.2';

# -- Replace OCR from last good backup
# -- May need to check $GI_HOME/logs/$HOST/client/ocrcheck*
# ./ocrconfig -restore backup00.ocr
# ./crsctl replace votedisk +OV
```

ACFS File System

> Tip: If you are not logged in as root, acfsutil may not be in your path.
> acfs is located in the /sbin directory. If you are logged in as oracle, you
> will have to add /sbin to your environment $PATH variable or fully qualify
> the path of the executable.

First, create the ASM Volume

```
ASMCMD [+] > volcreate -G DATA01 -s 1g vol_dba
ASMCMD [+] > volinfo -G DATA01 vol_dba

Diskgroup Name: DATA01

        Volume Name: VOL_DBA
        Volume Device: /dev/asm/vol_dba-377
        State: ENABLED
        Size (MB): 1024
        Resize Unit (MB): 32
        Redundancy: UNPROT
        Stripe Columns: 4
        Stripe Width (K): 128
        Usage:
        Mountpath:
```

Other volinfo syntax

```
ASMCMD [+] > volinfo -a
Diskgroup Name: DATA01

        Volume Name: VOL_DBA
        Volume Device: /dev/asm/vol_dba-255
        State: ENABLED
        Size (MB): 305152
        Resize Unit (MB): 1024
        Redundancy: UNPROT
        Stripe Columns: 4
        Stripe Width (K): 128
        Usage: ACFS
        Mountpath: /dba
```

Looking for specific volume information:

```
ASMCMD [+] > DATA01 -G DATA01 VOL_DBA
Diskgroup Name: DATA01

        Volume Name: VOL_DBA
        Volume Device: /dev/asm/vol_dba-255
        State: ENABLED
```

```
Size (MB): 305152
Resize Unit (MB): 1024
Redundancy: UNPROT
Stripe Columns: 4
Stripe Width (K): 128
Usage: ACFS
Mountpath: /dba
```

```
ASMCMD [+] > volinfo --show_diskgroup /dev/asm/vol_dba-255
DATA01
ASMCMD [+] > volinfo --show_volume /dev/asm/vol_dba-255
vol_dba
```

mkfs on the ASM Volume

```
# /sbin/mkfs -t acfs -n "DBA FS" /dev/asm/vol_dba-255

mkfs.acfs: version                = 12.1.0.1.0
mkfs.acfs: on-disk version        = 39.0
mkfs.acfs: volume                 = /dev/asm/vol_dba-255
mkfs.acfs: volume size            = 1073741824
mkfs.acfs: Format complete.
```

Or you can create an EXT3 file system

```
# mkfs -t ext3 /dev/asm/vol_dba-255
```

Remove an ACFS File system	acfsutil rmfs
Resize an ACFS File system	acfsutil size
View/Modify ACFS Tune-ables	acfsutil tune
Register with ACFS Registry (Cluster-wide fstab)	acfsutil registry

Register with OCR (Cluster-wide fstab)

```
# /sbin/acfsutil registry -f -a /dev/asm/vol_dba-255 /dba
acfsutil registry: mount point /dba successfully added to Oracle Registry
```

Mount the ACFS File System

```
# /bin/mount -t acfs /dev/asm/vol_dba-255 /dba
```

ACFS Info

```
# acfsutil info fs /dba
```

```
/dba
    ACFS Version: 12.1.0.1.0
    flags:        MountPoint,Available
    mount time:   Thu Sep  4 17:00:37 2014
    volumes:      1
    total size:   1073741824
    total free:   991641600
    primary volume: /dev/asm/vol_dba-377
        label:                DBA FS
        flags:                Primary,Available,ADVM
        on-disk version:      39.0
        allocation unit:      4096
        major, minor:         252, 193025
        size:                 1073741824
        free:                 991641600
        ADVM diskgroup        DATA
        ADVM resize increment: 33554432
        ADVM redundancy:      unprotected
        ADVM stripe columns:  4
        ADVM stripe width:    131072
    number of snapshots:  0
    snapshot space usage: 0
    replication status: DISABLED
```

fsck

```
# fsck -t acfs /dev/asm/vol_dba-255

fsck from util-linux-ng 2.17.2
version                  = 12.1.0.1.0
*******************************
********** Pass: 1 **********
*******************************
Oracle ASM Cluster File System (ACFS) On-Disk Structure Version: 39.0
ACFS file system created at: Thu Sep  4 16:57:11 2014
checking primary file system

        Files checked in primary file system: 100%


        Checking if any files are orphaned...


        0 orphans found

Checker completed with no errors.
```

Shrink the file system by 2G

In this example, we will shrink the file system by 2G down to 3G:

```
$ /sbin/acfsutil size -2G -d /dev/asm/vol_rpts-340
/apps/oracle/acfsmounts/data_vol_rpts
acfsutil size: new file system size: 3221225472 (3072MB)
```

Increase the file system by 2G

In this example, we will increase the file system by 2G and put the file system back to 5G.

```
$ /sbin/acfsutil size +2G -d /dev/asm/vol_rpts-340
/apps/oracle/acfsmounts/data_vol_rpts
acfsutil size: new file system size: 5368709120 (5120MB)
```

ACFS Snapshots

Create ACFS Snapshots

```
# acfsutil snap create mysnap_1 /dba/acfsdata/vol_dba
acfsutil snap create: Snapshot operation is complete.
```

Create ACFS Snapshot As Read only

```
# acfsutil snap create -r bkup_rosnap_1 /dba
acfsutil snap create: Snapshot operation is complete.
```

Delete ACFS Snapshots

```
# acfsutil snap delete mysnap_1 /dba/acfsdata/vol_dba
acfsutil snap delete: Snapshot operation is complete.
```

ACFS Dictionary Views

v$asm_acfs_encryption_info	Encryption information for each Oracle ACFS file system
v$asm_acfs_security_info	Security realm information for each Oracle ACFS file system

`v$asm_acfsvolumes`	Info about mounted Oracle ACFS volumes correlated with V$ASM_FILESYSTEM
`v$asm_volume` `v$asm_volume_stat`	ADVM volume information that is a part of an Oracle ASM instance
`v$asm_acfsvolumes`	Info about mounted Oracle ACFS volumes correlated with V$ASM_FILESYSTEM
`v$asm_filesystem`	Display information for every mounted Oracle ACFS file system

ACFS Snapshot Information

```
# acfsutil snap info /dba

snapshot name:                 bkup_rosnap_1
RO snapshot or RW snapshot:    RO
parent name:                   /dba
snapshot creation time:        Thu Sep  4 17:11:11 2014

    number of snapshots:  1
    snapshot space usage: 49152
```

Reverse Engineer ASMLIB Disks to Device Names with kfed

```
#!/bin/bash
for asmlibdisk in `ls /dev/oracleasm/disks/*`
do
  echo "ASMLIB disk name: $asmlibdisk"
  asmdisk=`kfed read $asmlibdisk | grep dskname | tr -s ' '| cut -f2 -d' '`
  echo "ASM disk name: $asmdisk"
  majorminor=`ls -l $asmlibdisk | tr -s ' ' | cut -f5,6 -d' '`
  device=`ls -l /dev | tr -s ' ' | grep "$majorminor" | cut -f10 -d' '`
  echo "Device path: /dev/$device"
done
```

Here's a sample output from this script:

```
ASMLIB disk name: /dev/oracleasm/disks/DATA1
ASM disk name: DATA1
Device path: /dev/sdb4
ASMLIB disk name: /dev/oracleasm/disks/DATA2
```

```
ASM disk name: DATA2
Device path: /dev/sdc1
ASMLIB disk name: /dev/oracleasm/disks/OCR1
ASM disk name: OCR1
Device path: /dev/sdb1
ASMLIB disk name: /dev/oracleasm/disks/OCR2
ASM disk name: OCR2
Device path: /dev/sdb2
ASMLIB disk name: /dev/oracleasm/disks/OCR3
ASM disk name: OCR3
Device path: /dev/sdb3
ASMLIB disk name: /dev/oracleasm/disks/RECO1
ASM disk name: RECO1
Device path: /dev/sdd1
```

KFOD

kfod is another ASM disk discovery utility executed from the operating system level and is located in the $GRID_HOME/bin directory. kfod is heavily leveraged during installation and by tools like OUI, DBCA and ASMCA.

List all active ASM instances in ASM cluster

```
kfod op=insts

--------------------------------------------------------------------------------
ORACLE_SID ORACLE_HOME
================================================================================
    +ASM1 /u01/app/12.1/grid
    +ASM2 /u01/app/12.1/grid
```

Display client databases accessing local ASM instance

```
$ kfod op=clients

--------------------------------------------------------------------------------
ORACLE_SID VERSION
================================================================================
  stgdb000 12.1.0.1.0
     +ASM1 12.1.0.1.0
     +ASM1 12.1.0.1.0
     +ASM1 12.1.0.1.0
   nishan1 12.1.0.1.0
   nishan1 12.1.0.1.0
 stgdb0021 12.1.0.1.0
   -MGMTDB 12.1.0.1.0
     +ASM2 12.1.0.1.0
     +ASM2 12.1.0.1.0
     +ASM2 12.1.0.1.0
   nishan2 12.1.0.1.0
```

```
   nishan2 12.1.0.1.0
 stgdb0022 12.1.0.1.0
```

The Linux blkid tool can also we used to obtain list of ASM member disks

```
#blkid| grep asm

/dev/emcpowerj1: LABEL="VOL4" TYPE="oracleasm"
/dev/emcpowerk1: LABEL="VOL3" TYPE="oracleasm"
/dev/emcpowerl1: LABEL="VOL2" TYPE="oracleasm"
/dev/emcpowerm1: LABEL="VOL1" TYPE="oracleasm"
/dev/emcpowern1: LABEL="VOL1" TYPE="oracleasm"
```

Display Disk Groups

```
$ kfod op=groups
```

```
---------------------------------------------------------------------
Group          Size          Free Redundancy Name
=====================================================================
   1:      51196 Mb      40516 Mb     EXTERN RECO
   2:      38399 Mb       7332 Mb     NORMAL OCR
   3:      63996 Mb      40952 Mb     EXTERN DATA
```

Display Disk Groups and Disks

```
$ kfod ds=true disks=all
```

```
---------------------------------------------------------------------
Disk        Size Path                          Disk Group   User    Group
=====================================================================
   1:     12800 Mb ORCL:DATA1                   DATA
   2:     51199 Mb ORCL:DATA2                   DATA
   3:     12799 Mb ORCL:OCR1                    OCR
   4:     12800 Mb ORCL:OCR2                    OCR
   5:     12800 Mb ORCL:OCR3                    OCR
   6:     51199 Mb ORCL:RECO1                   RECO
---------------------------------------------------------------------

ORACLE_SID ORACLE_HOME
=====================================================================
   +ASM1 /u01/app/12.1/grid
   +ASM2 /u01/app/12.1/grid
```

List All Disks

```
$ kfod disks=all
```

```
---------------------------------------------------------------------
Disk        Size Path
=====================================================================
   0      12800 Mb ORCL:DATA1
   1      51196 Mb ORCL:DATA2
```

```
[oracle@vnarac12c01a ~]$ kfod disks=all
--------------------------------------------------------------------------------
  Disk          Size Path                                      User    Group
================================================================================
    1:      12800 Mb ORCL:DATA1
    2:      51199 Mb ORCL:DATA2
    3:      12799 Mb ORCL:OCR1
    4:      12800 Mb ORCL:OCR2
    5:      12800 Mb ORCL:OCR3
    6:      51199 Mb ORCL:RECO1
--------------------------------------------------------------------------------
ORACLE_SID ORACLE_HOME
================================================================================
    +ASM1 /u01/app/12.1/grid
    +ASM2 /u01/app/12.1/grid
```

List Disks for the DATA Disk Group

```
$ kfod g=DATA

--------------------------------------------------------------------------------
  Disk          Size Path
================================================================================
    0       12800 Mb ORCL:DATA1
    1       51196 Mb ORCL:DATA2
```

Discover ASM Disks and Display Disk Header Include DG Name

```
$ kfod disks=asm status=true dscvgroup=true

--------------------------------------------------------------------------------
  Disk          Size Header    Path                            Disk Group   User
Group
================================================================================
    1:      12800 Mb MEMBER    ORCL:DATA1                      DATA
    2:      51199 Mb MEMBER    ORCL:DATA2                      DATA
    3:      12799 Mb MEMBER    ORCL:OCR1                       OCR
    4:      12800 Mb MEMBER    ORCL:OCR2                       OCR
    5:      12800 Mb MEMBER    ORCL:OCR3                       OCR
    6:      51199 Mb MEMBER    ORCL:RECO1                      RECO
--------------------------------------------------------------------------------
ORACLE_SID ORACLE_HOME
================================================================================
    +ASM1 /u01/app/12.1/grid
    +ASM2 /u01/app/12.1/grid
```

KFED

kfed is available from Oracle Database 11g Release 1 and forward and
can be used to read and write ASM metadata, in particular disk headers
and ASM metadata contents. kfed in write mode is a powerful but can be
potentially destructive tool in the wrong hands.

Read ASM Disk Header Block

```
$ sudo /u01/app/12.1/grid/bin/kfed read /dev/sdc2 |more
```

Read the Specified AU and Block Number

```
$ sudo /u01/app/12.1/grid/bin/kfed op=read dev=/dev/sdc1 aunum=3 blknum=3
|more
```

Read the Specified AU and Block Number Into a File

```
$ sudo /u01/app/12.1/grid/bin/kfed op=read dev=/dev/sdc1 aunum=3 blknum=3
text=/tmp/asm_block3.txt
```

Shell Script to Look at Certain Portion of ASM Disks

```
$ kfed read /dev/oracleasm/disks/DATA1 |egrep -i
"kfdhdb.hdrsts|kfdhdb.dskname|kfdhdb.grpname|kfdhdb.fgname|kfdhdb.secsize|blk
size|driver.provstr|kfdhdb.ausize"

cat <<!!
Legend:
kfdhdb.hdrsts - Status of disk
kfdhdb.dskname - Name of the disk
kfdhdb.grpname - Name of disk group the disk belongs to
kfdhdb.fgname - Name of failure group the disk belongs to
kfdhdb.secsize - Sector size of disk
kfdhdb.blksize - Blocksize of disk
kfdhdb.driver.provstr - Provision string for use with asm
kfdhdb.ausize - AU size
!!
```

Here's a sample output from this code example:

```
kfdhdb.driver.provstr:    ORCLDISKDATA1 ; 0x000: length=13
kfdhdb.hdrsts:                        3 ; 0x027: KFDHDR_MEMBER
kfdhdb.dskname:                   DATA1 ; 0x028: length=5
kfdhdb.grpname:                    DATA ; 0x048: length=4
kfdhdb.fgname:                    DATA1 ; 0x068: length=5
kfdhdb.secsize:                     512 ; 0x0b8: 0x0200
kfdhdb.blksize:                    4096 ; 0x0ba: 0x1000
kfdhdb.ausize:                  4194304 ; 0x0bc: 0x00400000
```

AMDU

The ASM Metadata Dump Utility (AMDU) utility is part of the Oracle Grid
Infrastructure distribution. AMDU is used to extract the available
metadata from one or more ASM disks and generate formatted output of

individual blocks. AMDU should only be used in coordination with Oracle Support.

AMDU also has the ability to extract one or more files from an unmounted diskgroup and write them to the OS file system. This dump output can be shipped to Oracle Support for analysis. Oracle Support can use the dump output to generate formatted block printouts. AMDU does not require the diskgroup to be mounted or the ASM instance to active.

AMDU performs three basic functions. A given execution of AMDU may perform one, two or all three of these functions.

1. Dump metadata from ASM disks to the OS file system for later analysis.
2. Extract the contents of an ASM file and write it to an OS file system even if the diskgroup is not mounted.
3. Print metadata blocks

Display Help

```
amdu -help
```

Certified Expert

Oracle Exadata Certified
Implementation Specialist

2 Oracle ASM 12c New Features

FlexCluster vs FlexASM

Show difference

A Flex Cluster is designed over HUB-LEAF topology to scale the Cluster to large number of nodes, literally 1000s of nodes. Hub nodes are very much similar to the standard cluster architecture, they are tightly coupled through a private interconnect and have direct access to shared storage. On the contrary, Leaf nodes are very light weight servers, not connected to other leaf nodes, and have no direct access to the storage. A Hub node can have multiple leaf nodes, but, a node leaf can't be part of multiple of Hub nodes. In a nutshell, the prime purpose of an Oracle Flex

Cluster is to provide the combined database and application tiers together in a single clustering environment.

Let's start the 12c Flex install, with the execution of the traditional runInstaller script

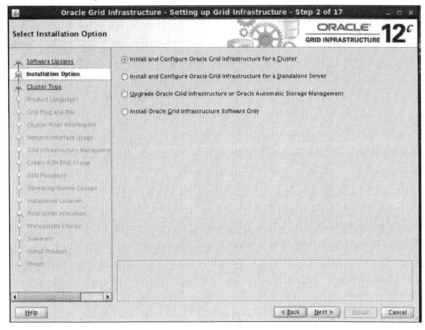

Let's choose Install 12c Flex Cluster

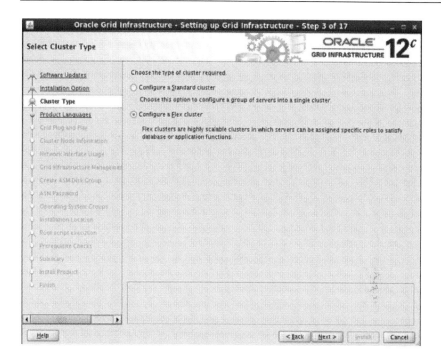

Now let's specify the Scan information and yes, we'll need to define GNS and since we have to use GNS, we'll need to get DNS domain delegation setup. In our case we have us.viscosityna-test.com as the sub-domain

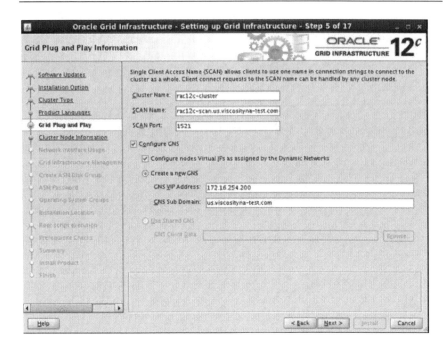

After this step, we see the new stuff!! We define which nodes in the cluster will be Hubs and which will be Leaf. Note, people will occasionally use the terms Hub and RIM interchangeably. It just historical.

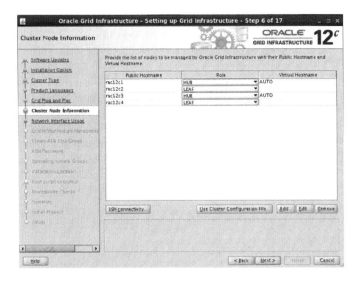

Let's specify the interfaces. You all have seen this screen before. But it now got a small twist to it. You can specify a separate "ASM &Private" networks. We will discuss ASM Networks in the FlexASM overview section.

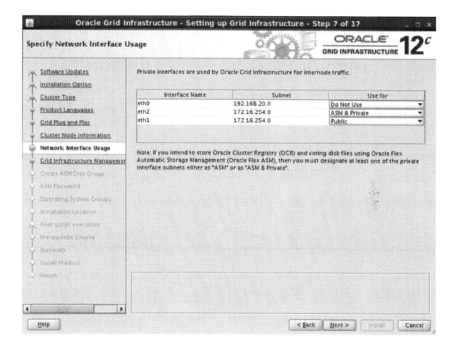

Now the validation!

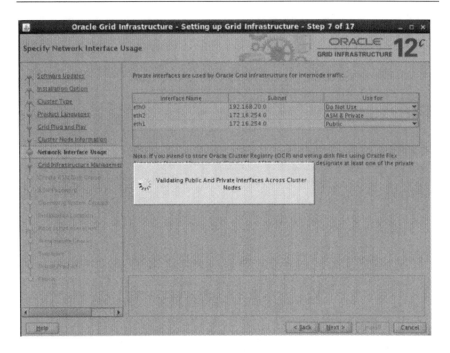

This step is new too. You have the option to configure Grid Infrastructure Repository, which is used for storing Cluster Health Monitor (CHM) data. In 11gR2 this was stored in a Berkley DB database and was created by default. Now this option allows users to specify a Oracle Database to store the CHM data. This database is a single instance database that is named MGMTDB by default. It is an internal CRS resource, which has HA-failover capabilities. We will cover this topic in more detail later, but we should mention that this is the only opportunity to create this repository; i,e, you have uninstall/reinstall to get this GI repos option.

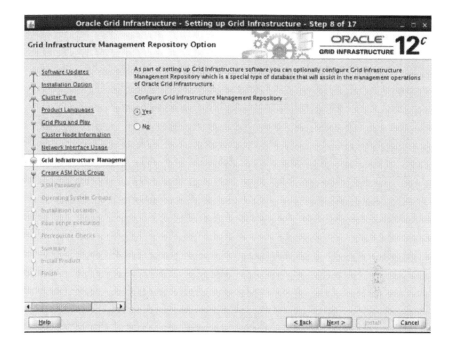

Now the fun stuff! Let's create the ASM disk group. Note, that if you are configuring a GI repo, then you will need a minimum of 5GB disk (for testers and laptop folks).

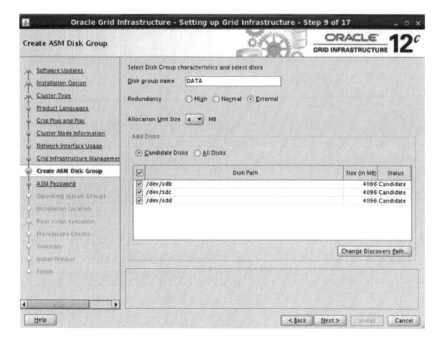

As in previous versions, the next set of steps we define passwords, specify IPMI or not, define the group definitions, and specify the Oracle Home and Oracle Base. In Oracle 12c, we can specify the root password/credentials, for downstream root required actions.

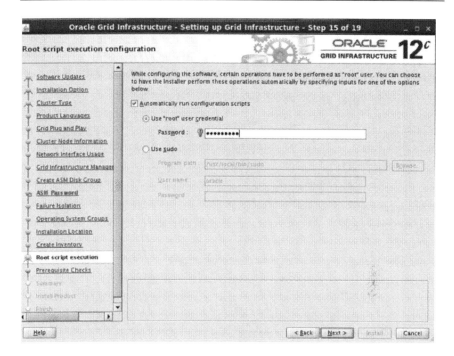

Run some fix some things, execute fixup.sh script

Finally we started the install.

ASM FlexASM configuration

In this section we will install a standard RAC configuration (non-FlexCluster); meaning all nodes are HUB nodes. In this configuration we have the option to specify a Flex ASM configuration

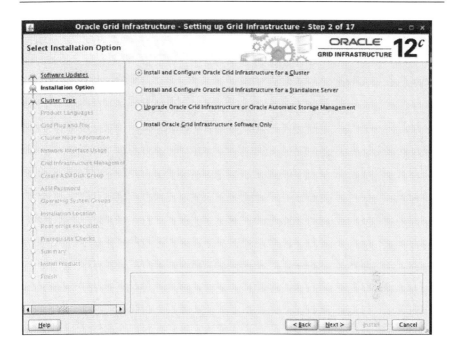

We specify Standard Cluster

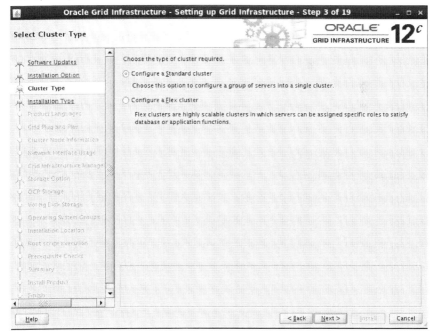

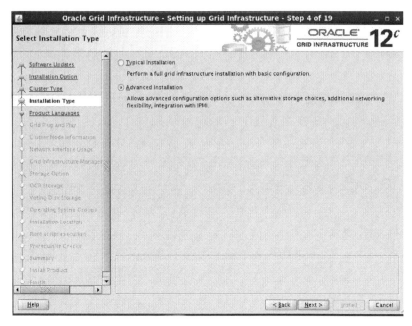

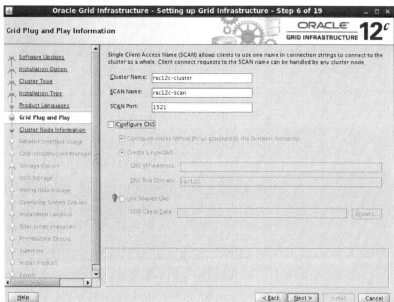

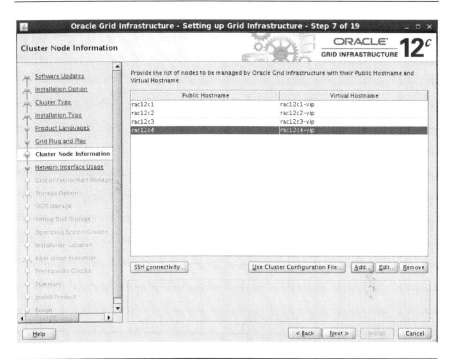

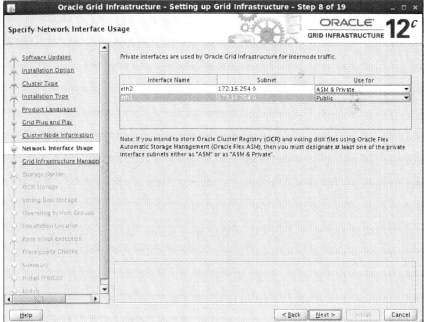

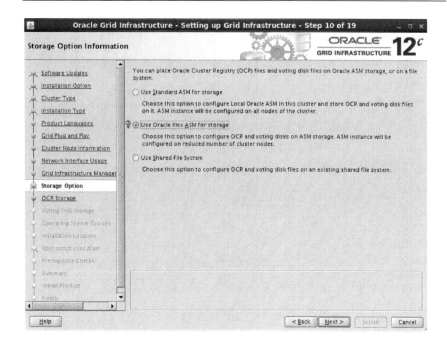

Above we installed and configured FlexASM and a CDB plus a couple of PDBs. Also, this was Policy Managed with a cardinality of 2. Now let's see what the configuration looks like, and we can break it down using the wonderful crsctl and srvctl tools. First let's ensure we are really running in FlexASM mode:

```
$ asmcmd showclustermode
ASM cluster : Flex mode enabled


[oracle@rac02 ~]$ srvctl status   serverpool -serverpool naboo
Server pool name: naboo
Active servers count: 2


[oracle@rac01 trace]$ crsctl get node role status -all
Node 'rac01' active role is 'hub'
Node 'rac03' active role is 'hub'
Node 'rac02' active role is 'hub'
Node 'rac04' active role is 'hub'


[oracle@rac01 ~]$ crsctl stat res -t
--------------------------------------------------------------------------
Name          Target  State        Server               State details
```

```
--------------------------------------------------------------------------------
Local Resources
--------------------------------------------------------------------------------
ora.ASMNET1LSNR_ASM.lsnr
               ONLINE   ONLINE        rac01                        STABLE
               ONLINE   ONLINE        rac02                        STABLE
               ONLINE   ONLINE        rac03                        STABLE
               ONLINE   ONLINE        rac04                        STABLE
```

You notice that we have 4 ASM listeners one on each node in the Cluster. You will see the process as the following on each node:

```
$ ps -ef |grep -i asmnet

ooracle    6646     1  0 12:19 ?        00:00:00 /u01/app/12.1.0/grid/bin/tnslsnr
ASMNET1LSNR_ASM -no_crs_notify -inherit

ora.CRSDATA.DATAVOL1.advm
               ONLINE   ONLINE        rac01                        Volume device /dev/a
                                                                   sm/datavol1-194 is o
                                                                   nline,STABLE
               ONLINE   ONLINE        rac02                        Volume device /dev/a
                                                                   sm/datavol1-194 is o
                                                                   nline,STABLE
               ONLINE   OFFLINE       rac03                        Unable to connect to
                                                                   ASM,STABLE
               ONLINE   ONLINE        rac04                        Volume device /dev/a
                                                                   sm/datavol1-194 is o
                                                                   nline,STABLE
```

The datavol1 ADVM resource runs on all the nodes where indicated it should run. In this case we see that RAC03 is having some issues. We like the fact crsctl tells something is amiss here on node3

```
ora.CRSDATA.dg
               ONLINE    ONLINE        rac01                        STABLE
               ONLINE    ONLINE        rac02                        STABLE
               ONLINE    ONLINE        rac03                        STABLE
               OFFLINE   OFFLINE       rac04                        STABLE


ora.FRA.dg
               ONLINE    ONLINE        rac01                        STABLE
               ONLINE    ONLINE        rac02                        STABLE
               ONLINE    ONLINE        rac03                        STABLE
               OFFLINE   OFFLINE       rac04                        STABLE


The crsdata and fra disk groups resource is started on all nodes except node
4
```

```
ora.LISTENER.lsnr
                ONLINE   ONLINE        rac01                     STABLE
                ONLINE   ONLINE        rac02                     STABLE
                ONLINE   ONLINE        rac03                     STABLE
                ONLINE   ONLINE        rac04                     STABLE
```

We all know, as in 11gR2, that this is the Node listener.

```
ora.PDBDATA.dg
                ONLINE   ONLINE        rac01                     STABLE
                ONLINE   ONLINE        rac02                     STABLE
                ONLINE   ONLINE        rac03                     STABLE
                OFFLINE  OFFLINE       rac04                     STABLE
```

The pdbdata disk groups resource is started on all nodes except node 4.

```
ora.crsdata.datavol1.acfs
                ONLINE   ONLINE        rac01              mounted on /u02/app/
                                                          oracle/acfsmounts,ST
                                                          ABLE
                ONLINE   ONLINE        rac02              mounted on /u02/app/
                                                          oracle/acfsmounts,ST
                                                          ABLE
                ONLINE   OFFLINE       rac03              (2) volume /u02/app/
                                                          oracle/acfsmounts of
                                                          fline,STABLE
                ONLINE   ONLINE        rac04              mounted on /u02/app/
                                                          oracle/acfsmounts,ST
                                                          ABLE
```

ACFS filesystem resource for datavol1 is started on all nodes except node3. But we think the following has something to do with it. We need to debug this a bit later. We even tried:

```
$ asmcmd volenable --all
ASMCMD-9470: ASM proxy instance unavailable
ASMCMD-9471: cannot enable or disable volumes

ora.net1.network
                ONLINE   ONLINE        rac01                     STABLE
                ONLINE   ONLINE        rac02                     STABLE
                ONLINE   ONLINE        rac03                     STABLE
                ONLINE   ONLINE        rac04                     STABLE
ora.ons
                ONLINE   ONLINE        rac01                     STABLE
                ONLINE   ONLINE        rac02                     STABLE
                ONLINE   ONLINE        rac03                     STABLE
                ONLINE   ONLINE        rac04                     STABLE
```

The Network (in this case we only have only Net1) and ONS are same as in previous versions.

```
ora.proxy_advm
                ONLINE   ONLINE        rac01                    STABLE
                ONLINE   ONLINE        rac02                    STABLE
                ONLINE   OFFLINE       rac03                    STABLE
                ONLINE   ONLINE        rac04                    STABLE
```

Since proxy_advm is not started on node3, the file systems will not come online but again, we will look at that later.

```
--------------------------------------------------------------------------
Cluster Resources
--------------------------------------------------------------------------
ora.LISTENER_SCAN1.lsnr
      1         ONLINE   ONLINE        rac02              STABLE
ora.LISTENER_SCAN2.lsnr
      1         ONLINE   ONLINE        rac03              STABLE
ora.LISTENER_SCAN3.lsnr
      1         ONLINE   ONLINE        rac04              STABLE
ora.MGMTLSNR
      1         ONLINE   ONLINE        rac01              169.254.90.36 172.16
                                                         .11.10,STABLE
ora.asm
      1         ONLINE   ONLINE        rac03              STABLE
      2         ONLINE   ONLINE        rac01              STABLE
      3         ONLINE   ONLINE        rac02              STABLE
```

Since we have the cardinality of 3 ASM instance we have 3 ASM resources active.

```
ora.cvu
      1         ONLINE   ONLINE        rac01              STABLE
ora.mgmtdb
      1         ONLINE   ONLINE        rac01              Open,STABLE
ora.oc4j
      1         ONLINE   ONLINE        rac01              STABLE
ora.rac01.vip
      1         ONLINE   ONLINE        rac01              STABLE
ora.rac02.vip
      1         ONLINE   ONLINE        rac02              STABLE
ora.rac03.vip
      1         ONLINE   ONLINE        rac03              STABLE
ora.rac04.vip
      1         ONLINE   ONLINE        rac04              STABLE
ora.scan1.vip
      1         ONLINE   ONLINE        rac02              STABLE
ora.scan2.vip
```

1	ONLINE	ONLINE	rac03		STABLE
ora.scan3.vip					
1	ONLINE	ONLINE	rac04		STABLE
ora.tatooine.db					
1	ONLINE	ONLINE	rac01		Open, STABLE
2	ONLINE	ONLINE	rac02		Open, STABLE

As we stated above, we specified a Policy Managed database with cardinality of 2, so we have 2 database instances running. Here's some other important supporting info on FlexASM:

```
[oracle@rac02 ~]$ srvctl config asm -detail
ASM home: /u01/app/12.1.0/grid
Password file: +CRSDATA/orapwASM
ASM listener: LISTENER
ASM is enabled.
ASM instance count: 3
Cluster ASM listener: ASMNET1LSNR_ASM


[oracle@rac02 ~]$ srvctl status  filesystem
ACFS file system /u02/app/oracle/acfsmounts is mounted on nodes
rac01, rac02, rac04
```

Here is what the Database has to say about FlexASM

```
NOTE: ASMB registering with ASM instance as client 0x10001 (reg:1377584805)
NOTE: ASMB connected to ASM instance +ASM1 (Flex mode; client id 0x10001)
NOTE: ASMB rebuilding ASM server state
NOTE: ASMB rebuilt 2 (of 2) groups
SUCCESS: ASMB reconnected & completed ASM server state
```

So for the interesting part. You will notice that ASM is not running node 4:

```
[oracle@rac02 ~]$ srvctl status  asm -v

ASM is running on rac01, rac02, rac03
[oracle@rac02 ~]$ srvctl status  asm -detail
ASM is running on rac01, rac02, rac03
```

So, how does a client (ocrdump, rman, asmcmd, etc..) connect to if ASM if there is no ASM on that node. You notice that a pipe is created, a connect string is generated and passed to ASMCMD to connect remotely to ASM2 on node2!

```
22-Sep-13 12:54 ASMCMD Foreground (PID = 14106):  Pipe /tmp/pipe_14106 has
been found.
22-Sep-13 12:54 ASMCMD Background (PID = 14117):  Successfully opened the
pipe /tmp/pipe_14106
22-Sep-13 12:54 ASMCMD Foreground (PID = 14106):  Successfully opened the
pipe /tmp/pipe_14106 in read mode
NOTE: Executing kfod /u01/app/12.1.0/grid/bin/kfod op=getclstype..
22-Sep-13 12:54 Printing the connection string
contype =
driver =
<dbi:Oracle:(DESCRIPTION=(TRANSPORT_CONNECT_TIMEOUT=1)(EXPIRE_TIME=1)(ADDRESS
_LIST=(SECURITY=(AUTHENTICATION_SERVICES=NTS))(ADDRESS=(PROTOCOL=tcp)(HOST=17
2.16.11.10)(PORT=1521))(ADDRESS=(PROTOCOL=tcp)(HOST=172.16.11.11)(PORT=1521))
(ADDRESS=(PROTOCOL=tcp)(HOST=172.16.11.13)(PORT=1521)))(CONNECT_DATA=(SERVICE
_NAME=+ASM)))>
instanceName = <>
usr = <crsuser__asm_001>
ServiceName = <+ASM>
23-Sep-13 16:23 Successfully connected to ASM instance +ASM2
23-Sep-13 16:23 NOTE: Querying ASM instance to get list of disks
22-Sep-13 12:54 Registered Daemon process.
22-Sep-13 12:54 ASMCMD Foreground (PID = 14106):  Closed pipe
/tmp/pipe_14106.
```

Fundamental New Features

- Increase maximum number of Disk Groups to 511 (Previous limit was 63)
- ASMCMD Command for renaming ASM Disk
- ASM instance Patch-level verification
- Patch level verification is disabled during rolling patches
- Replicated Physical Metadata
- Improves reliability
- Virtual Metadata has always been replicated with ASM mirroring
- Largest disk size beyond 2T (support 32P)

12c Convert from Standard Mode to Flex mode

```
$ asmca -silent -convertToFlexASM -asmNetworks eth1/192.168.0.1 -
asmListenerPort 1521

$ $ORACLE_BASE/cfgtoollogs/asmca/scripts/converttoFlexASM.sh
```

```
$ asmcmd showclustermode
ASM cluster : Flex mode enabled
```

> **NOTES:**
> - FlexASM eliminates requirement for an ASM instance on every cluster node
> - Databases can connect to any available ASM instance
> - Database instances can failover to a secondary ASM instance
> - Option to perform maintenance on ASM without need to stop the RAC databases
> - Administrators specify the cardinality of ASM instances (default is 3)
> - Clusterware ensures ASM cardinality is maintained

12c orapwd passwd file Inside ASM

In releases prior Oracle 12c, most of the Oracle database and ASM related files could be stored in ASM disk groups. The key exception was the password file, both the ASM and database password files. This password file, created by orapwd utility, was created in the $ORACLE_HOME/dbs directory by default and thus was local to the node and instance. This required manual synchronization of the password files. If the password file became out of sync between instances, it could cause inconsistent login behavior. Although Oracle 11gR2 provided the capability for cross-instance calls (CIC) to synchronize the password file, if an instance or node was inactive, then synchronization was not possible, still leaving the password file. Inconsistent ASM password files is more problematic for ASM instances, since ASM does not have a data dictionary.

In Oracle 12c (for new installations), the default location of the password file is in ASM. The location of the password file becomes an CRS resource attribute of the ASM and database instance. The ASM instance and disk group that is storing the password file needs to be available before password file authentication is possible for the database. The SYSASM or SYDBA privilege can be used password file in ASM.

For the ASM instance, operating system authentication is performed to bootstrap the startup of the ASM instance. This is transparently handled as part of the Grid Infrastructure startup sequence. As in previous releases, the SYSASM privilege is required to create the ASM password file.

Note that the compatible.asm disk group attribute must be set to 12.1 or later to enable storage of shared password files in an ASM disk group.

```
$ orapwd file='+CRSDATA'  dbuniqueue='prod' password='oracle123'
$ orapwd asm=y file='+CRSDATA'  password='asmoracle123'

ASMCMD [+] > pwget --asm
+CRSDATA/orapwASM
```

12c Fast Resync Feature

The Oracle 11g Disk online feature, which has been available since 11gR1, provides the capability to online and resync disks that have incurred transient failures. Note, this feature is applicable only to ASM disk groups that use ASM redundancy.

The resync operation essentially updates the ASM extents that were modified while the disk or disks were offline. However, prior to Oracle 12c, this feature was single threaded; i.e., effectively using a single process to bring the disk(s) completely online. For disks that have been offline for a prolonged period of time, combined with a large number of extent changes, could make the disk resync operation very long. In Oracle 12c, this online and resync operation becomes a multi-threaded operation very similar to the ASM rebalance operation.
Thus the disk online can leverage a power level from 1 to 1024, with 1 being the default. This power level controls how many outstanding IOs will be issued to the IO subsystem, and has a direct impact to the

performance of the system. Keep in mind that you are still bounded by the server's IO subsystem layer, thus setting a very large power level does not necessarily improve resync time. This is because a server where the resync operation is submitted can only process a certain number of IOs; similarly, a disk can only can a limited number of concurrent IO operations. A power level between 8-16 is been proven beneficial for resync-ing a single disk, whereas a power level of 8-64 has been proven useful for bringing a failure group (with multiple disks) online.

In versions prior to Oracle 12c , the resync operation sets and clears flags [in Staleness Registry] at the begin and end of resync operation, an interrupted resync operation would need to be started from the beginning since the stale extent bit flags are cleared at the end of the resync operation. In 12c ASM, resync operations now support checkpoints. These checkpoints are now set after each batch of extents are updated and their stale extent flags cleared, thus making auto-restart began at the last checkpoint. If the resync operation fails or gets interrupted, it is automatically restarted from the last resync phase and using internally generated resync checkpoints.

```
SQL> alter diskgroup reco online disk reco_0004 power 16;

ASMCMD> online -G reco -D reco_004 -power 16
```

NOTES:

1. Allows Admins to throttle the resync operation
2. Power limit can be set for disk resync operations from 1 to 1024

12c Fast Disk Replacement

```
SQL> alter diskgroup replace disk rec_0004 with '/dev/mapper/mpathe'
```

NOTES:

- 12c ASM allows fast, low-overhead replacement of failed disks
- Replace new disk in same slot as failed disk
- Replacement disk takes the same name as the original disk

12c Failure Group Repair Timer

```
SQL> alter diskgroup reco set attribute 'failgroup_repair_time = 36h';
```

NOTES:

- Useful for protecting against transient failgroup issues, such as controller issues or poor connectivity in Stretch Clusters
- New disk group attribute, failgroup_repair_time
- Similar to existing disk repair time
- Default setting is 24 hours

12c Data Scrubbing

```
SQL> alter diskgroup data set attribute 'content.check' = 'TRUE'
Requires content.check attribute to enable
```

or

```
SQL> alter diskgroup data scrub repair;
SQL> alter diskgroup data scrub disk data_0004 norepair power high;
```

NOTES:

Scrubbing can be performed on a Disk Group, on individual files or individual disks

12c Rebalance Improvements

```
EXPLAIN WORK FOR ALTER DISKGROUP pdata DROP DISK pdata_0008;
Explained.

SELECT est_work FROM V$ASM_ESTIMATE;
EST_WORK
--------
    2244
```

ASM Network

In versions prior to 12c, Oracle Clusterware required a public network for client application access and a private network for inter-node communication within the cluster, this included ASM traffic. With Flex ASM Network feature also provides the capability to isolate ASM's internal network traffic to its own dedicated private network. The OUI presents the DBA with the choice as to whether a dedicated network is to be used for ASM. The ASM network is the communication path in which all the traffic between database instances and ASM instances commence. This traffic is mostly the metadata such as a particular file's extent map. If the customer chooses, the ASM private network can be dedicated for ASM traffic or shared with CSS and a dedicated network is not required.

The key benefits of Flex ASM Network features includes the following:
- Eliminates requirement for an ASM instance on every cluster server
- Database instances connects to any ASM instance in the cluster
- Database instances can failover to a secondary ASM instance
- Administrators specify the cardinality of ASM instances (default is 3)
- Clusterware ensures ASM cardinality is maintained

ACFS 12c (aka CloudFS)

1. Oracle databases created on CloudFS can leverage snapshots (RW,RO)
2. Both provide equivalent performance
3. Set stripe columns to 1 for the ADVM volume
4. Disables ADVM volume striping
5. Set FILESYSTEMIO_OPTIONS=SETALL in the database init.ora
6. Enables direct I/O for the database, bypassing the OS file system

cache

Move a database instance from one ASM instance connection to another

```
SQL> alter system relocate client 'tatooine_1:tatooine';


System altered.
```

ASM / ACFS Supporting Information

```
$ srvctl config asm -detail
ASM home: /u01/app/12.1.0/grid
Password file: +CRSDATA/orapwASM
ASM listener: LISTENER
ASM is enabled.
ASM instance count: 3
Cluster ASM listener: ASMNET1LSNR_ASM

ACFS is also enabled for storing trace data

$ srvctl status  filesystem
ACFS file system /u02/app/oracle/acfsmounts is mounted on nodes
rac01,rac02,rac04

$ srvctl status asm -proxy
ADVM proxy is running on node rac01,rac02,rac03,rac04
```

Oracle 12c ASM Optimizations on Engineered Systems

In Chapter 12, we described some of the ASM optimizations that were made specifically for Engineered Systems like Exadata and Oracle Database Appliance (ODA). There are several other important features in Oracle 12c ASM to support of engineered systems, This section describes further ASM optimizations and features added in Oracle 12c for supporting Engineered Systems.

- **Exadata Copy offload** - With Oracle Database 12c, intra- extent relocations performed by a rebalance operation can be offloaded to Exadata Storage Server. Using this capability, a single offload request can replace multiple read and write I/O requests. Offloading relocations avoids sending data to the ASM host, improving rebalance performance. Mainly intra-disk relocations are offloaded

- **Fast disk replacement -** In versions 11gR2 and prior, a failed disk would become offlined/dropped, then a new disk replaced (generally in the same tray slot), and finally this disk is added back into the ASM disk group using. This requires a complete diskgroup rebalance. In Oracle 12c, the Fast Disk Replacement feature allows a failed disk(s) to be replaced without requiring a complete diskgroup rebalance operation. With the Fast Disk Replacement feature, the disk is replaced in the disk tray slot, and the added back into the ASM disk group as a *replacement disk*. Initially this disk is in an offline state and resync'ed (populated) with copies of ASM extents from mirror extents from its partners. Note, that since this is a replacement disk, it inherits the same disk name and automatically back into the same failure group. The key benefit of Fast Disk Replacement feature is that it allows ASM Administrators to replace a disk as a fast, efficient, atomic operation with minimal system impact, since no disk group reorganization is necessary

The main difference between Fast Disk Resync (discussed earlier) and Fast Disk replacement is that the disk has failed and implicity dropped in Fast Disk replacement case; whereas in Fast Disk Resync the disk is temporarily offline due to a transient path or component failure.

Failure Group Repair Timer - When individual disk fails, the failure is often terminal and the disk must be replaced. When all the disks in a Failure Group fail simultaneously, it is unlikely that all the disks individually failed at the same time. Rather it is more likely that some transient issue caused the failure. For example, a Failure Group could fail because of a storage network outage. Because Failure Group outages are more likely to be transient in nature, and because replacing all the disks in a Failure Group is far more expensive operation than replacing a single disk, it makes sense for Failure Groups to have a larger repair time to ensure that all the disks don't get dropped automatically in the event of a Failure Group outage. Administrators can now specify a Failure Group repair time similar to 11g disk repair timer, this includes a new disk group attribute called failgroup_repair_time. The default setting is 24 hours.

ASM Real World Solutions

Performing a High Level ASM Health Check

```
$ cat asmcheck.ksh
#!/bin/ksh
HOST=`hostname`
ASM_OS_DEV_NM=/tmp/asmdevicenames.log
ASMVOTEDSK=/tmp/asm_votingdisks.log
GRID_HOME=`cat /etc/oratab |grep "+ASM" |awk -F ":" '{print $2}'`
ORACLE_HOME=$GRID_HOME
PATH=$ORACLE_HOME/bin:$PATH:
export GAWK=/bin/gawk

#
#
do_pipe ()
{
    SQLP="$GRID_HOME/bin/sqlplus  -s / as sysdba";
    $SQLP |&      # Open a pipe to SQL*Plus
        print -p -- 'set feed off pause off pages 0 head off veri off line
500';
        print -p -- 'set term off time off';
        print -p -- "set sqlprompt ''";

        print -p -- 'select sysdate from dual;';
        read  -p SYSDATE;

        print -p -- "select version from v\$instance;";
        read  -p ASM_VERSION;

        print -p -- "select value from v\$parameter where name
='processes';";
        read  -p ASM_PROCESS;
        print -p -- "select value from v\$parameter where name
='asm_diskstring';";
        read  -p ASM_DISKSTRING;
        print -p -- "select value from v\$parameter where name
='asm_diskgroups';";
        read  -p ASM_DISKGROUPS;

        print -p -- "select value/1024/1024 from v\$parameter where
name='memory_target';";
        read  -p ASM_MEMORY;
        print -p -- "select value from v\$parameter where name
='sga_target';";
        read  -p ASM_SGA_TARGET;

        print -p -- "quit;";
```

```
        sleep 5;
}
#

function get_asminfo {
for LUNS in `ls /dev/oracleasm/disks/*`
do

 echo "ASMLIB disk: $LUNS"
 asmdisk=`kfed read $LUNS | grep dskname | tr -s ' ' | cut -f2 -d' '`
 echo "ASM disk: $asmdisk"

 majorminor=`ls -l $LUNS | tr -s ' ' | cut -f5,6 -d' '`
 dev=`ls -l /dev | tr -s ' ' | grep "$majorminor" | cut -f10 -d' '`
 echo "Device path: /dev/$dev"
 echo "----"

done

echo ""
echo "# ------------------------------------------------------ #";
/usr/sbin/oracleasm-discover;

}

function get_mem_info {
MEM=`free | $GAWK '/^Mem:/{ print int( ($2 / 1024 / 1024 + 4) / 4 ) * 4 }'`
SWAP=`free | $GAWK '/^Swap:/{ print int ( $2 / 1024 / 1024 + 0.5 ) }'`
HUGEPAGES=`grep HugePages_Total /proc/meminfo | $GAWK '{print $2}'`

echo "Physical Memory: $MEM          |Swap:  $SWAP"
echo "HugePages:  $HUGEPAGES"
}

export ORACLE_SID=`cat /etc/oratab |grep "+ASM" |awk -F ":" '{print $1}'`
CHKPMON=`ps -ef|grep -v grep|grep pmon_$i|awk '{print $8}'`
    if [ -n "$CHKPMON" ]; then
        do_pipe $ORACLE_SID

echo "# ------------------------------------------------------ #";
        echo "HOSTNAME:  ${HOST}"
        echo "GRID HOME:  ${GRID_HOME}"
        echo "ASM VERSION:  ${ASM_VERSION}"
        echo "ASM PROCESSES:  ${ASM_PROCESS}"
        echo "ASM MEMORY_TARGET: ${ASM_MEMORY} MB"
        echo "ASM SGA_TARGET: ${ASM_SGA_TARGET} MB"
        echo "ASM DISKSTRING: ${ASM_DISKSTRING}"
        echo "ASM DISKGROUPS: ${ASM_DISKGROUPS}"
echo "# ------------------------------------------------------ #";
        get_mem_info
echo "# ------------------------------------------------------ #";
    else
```

```
            echo "${ORACLE_SID} is not running."
     fi

echo "# ----------------------------------------------------------- #";
echo "LINUX VERSION INFORMATION:"
echo " "

[ -f "/etc/redhat-release" ] && cat /etc/redhat-release
[ -f "/etc/oracle-release" ] && cat /etc/oracle-release

uname -a

echo "# ----------------------------------------------------------- #";

##SQLP="sqlplus  -s / as sysdba";
##$SQLP <<! > $ASM_OS_DEV_NM
##set feed off pause off head on veri off line 500;
##set term off time off numwidth 15;
##set sqlprompt '';
##col label for a25
##col path for a55
##--select label,path,os_mb from v\$asm_disk;
##select label,os_mb from v\$asm_disk;
##exit;
##!

echo "ASM OS DEVICE INFORMATION:"
##cat $ASM_OS_DEV_NM
## Check for ASMLib

ASMLIBCHK=`rpm -qa |grep oracleasmlib`

if  [[ -n $ASMLIBCHK ]]
then
echo "# ----------------------------------------------------------- #";

   echo "ASMLIB RPM:  ${ASMLIBCHK}"
   echo " "
   ##echo "ASM OS DEVICE INFORMATION:"
   ##echo " "
       get_asminfo
else
   echo "ASMLIB is NOT installed."
fi

echo "# ----------------------------------------------------------- #";

## Check OCR/Voting disks
OCR=`$GRID_HOME/bin/ocrcheck |grep "Device/File Name" |awk '{print $4}'`
##echo " "
##echo "GRID HOME is located at ${GRID_HOME}."
```

```
echo "OCR LOCATION:  ${OCR}"
echo "# ------------------------------------------------------------ #";
echo " "

## Voting disk
$GRID_HOME/bin/crsctl query css votedisk > $ASMVOTEDSK

echo "VOTING DISK INFORMATION:"
echo " "
cat $ASMVOTEDSK
echo "# ------------------------------------------------------------ #";

## Cleanup
if [[ -f $ASM_OS_DEV_NM ]]
then
   rm $ASM_OS_DEV_NM
fi

if [[ -f $ASMVOTEDSK ]]
then
   rm $ASMVOTEDSK
fi
```

Here's a sample output from this script:

```
"# ------------------------------------------------------------
HOSTNAME:  vnarac12c01a.viscosityna.com
GRID HOME:  /u01/app/12.1/grid
ASM VERSION:  12.1.0.1.0
ASM PROCESSES:  120
ASM DISKSTRING: ORCL:*
ASM DISKGROUPS: DATA, RECO
ASM MEMORY_TARGET: 1024 MB
ASM SGA_TARGET:
"# ------------------------------------------------------------
Physical Memory:  8          |Swap:  6
HugePages:  0
"# ------------------------------------------------------------
"# ------------------------------------------------------------
LINUX VERSION INFORMATION:

Red Hat Enterprise Linux Server release 6.5 (Santiago)
Oracle Linux Server release 6.5
Linux vnarac12c01a.viscosityna.com 2.6.32-431.el6.x86_64 #1 SMP Wed Nov 20
23:56:07 PST 2013 x86_64 x86_64 x86_64 GNU/Linux
"# ------------------------------------------------------------
ASM OS DEVICE INFORMATION:
"# ------------------------------------------------------------
ASMLIB RPM:  oracleasmlib-2.0.4-1.el6.x86_64

ASMLIB disk: /dev/oracleasm/disks/DATA1
ASM disk: DATA1
```

```
Device path: /dev/sdb4
----
ASMLIB disk: /dev/oracleasm/disks/DATA2
ASM disk: DATA2
Device path: /dev/sdc1
----
ASMLIB disk: /dev/oracleasm/disks/OCR1
ASM disk: OCR1
Device path: /dev/sdb1
----
ASMLIB disk: /dev/oracleasm/disks/OCR2
ASM disk: OCR2
Device path: /dev/sdb2
----
ASMLIB disk: /dev/oracleasm/disks/OCR3
ASM disk: OCR3
Device path: /dev/sdb3
----
ASMLIB disk: /dev/oracleasm/disks/RECO1
ASM disk: RECO1
Device path: /dev/sdd1
----


"# ------------------------------------------------------------
Using ASMLib from /opt/oracle/extapi/64/asm/orcl/1/libasm.so
[ASM Library - Generic Linux, version 2.0.4 (KABI_V2)]
Discovered disk: ORCL:DATA1 [26214400 blocks (13421772800 bytes), maxio 512]
Discovered disk: ORCL:DATA2 [104857568 blocks (53687074816 bytes), maxio 512]
Discovered disk: ORCL:OCR1 [26214368 blocks (13421756416 bytes), maxio 512]
Discovered disk: ORCL:OCR2 [26214400 blocks (13421772800 bytes), maxio 512]
Discovered disk: ORCL:OCR3 [26214400 blocks (13421772800 bytes), maxio 512]
Discovered disk: ORCL:RECO1 [104857568 blocks (53687074816 bytes), maxio 512]
"# ------------------------------------------------------------
OCR LOCATION:  +OCR
"# ------------------------------------------------------------

VOTING DISK INFORMATION:

##  STATE    File Universal Id                 File Name Disk group
--  -----    ----------------                  --------- ---------
 1. ONLINE   0e499404d40d4fa2bff22a2457fff453  (ORCL:OCR1) [OCR]
 2. ONLINE   b8386e95642a4f47bf2cf1716958e0a0  (ORCL:OCR2) [OCR]
 3. ONLINE   35470782d3084f34bf395c6efb503b6b  (ORCL:OCR3) [OCR]
Located 3 voting disk(s).
"# ------------------------------------------------------------
```

Converting Exadata High Redundancy Disk Group to Normal Redundancy

We have been involved in several Exadata implementations where Oracle delivered the wrong ASM redundancy type to a customer. The customer expected single mirroring (normal redundancy) and lot more TBs of useable storage than what was delivered. We have a general rule; if you have to do it more than once, you better script it and automate it. Check out the script the we used to migrate an Exadata customer from high redundancy to normal redundancy.

```
define DG='&1'
set pages 0
set lines 200 trims on feed off  echo off echo off ver off
spool cr_&DG..sql
prompt CREATE DISKGROUP &DG NORMAL REDUNDANCY

set serveroutput on size unlimited

declare
v_failgroup v$asm_disk.failgroup%TYPE;

cursor c1 is
select chr(39)||path||chr(39) path, name
from v$asm_disk
where group_number = (select group_number from v$asm_diskgroup
                      where name=upper('&DG'))
and failgroup=v_failgroup
order by path;

cursor c2 is
select distinct failgroup
from v$asm_disk
order by failgroup;

cursor c3 is
select allocation_unit_size, compatibility, database_compatibility
from v$asm_diskgroup;
r3 c3%ROWTYPE;

begin
for r2 in c2 loop
v_failgroup := r2.failgroup;
dbms_output.put_line('FAILGROUP '||r2.failgroup||' DISK');

for r1 in c1 loop
if c1%rowcount = 1 then
   dbms_output.put_line(r1.path);
else
   dbms_output.put_line(','||r1.path);
end if;
```

```
end loop;

end loop;

open c3; fetch c3 into r3;
dbms_output.put_line('ATTRIBUTE');
dbms_output.put_line(chr(39)||'compatible.asm'||chr(39)||'='||chr(39)||r3.com
patibility||chr(39)||',');
dbms_output.put_line(chr(39)||'compatible.rdbms'||chr(39)||'='||chr(39)||r3.d
atabase_compatibility||chr(39)||',');
dbms_output.put_line(chr(39)||'au_size'||chr(39)||'='||chr(39)||r3.allocation
_unit_size||chr(39)||',');
dbms_output.put_line(chr(39)||'cell.smart_scan_capable'||chr(39)||'='||chr(39
)||'TRUE'||chr(39)||';');
close c3;

end;
/
spool off
```

Here's a sample of the generated script for the DATA disk group.

```
CREATE DISKGROUP DATA_EXAD NORMAL REDUNDANCY
FAILGROUP EXADCEL01 DISK
'o/10.0.0.3/DATA_EXAD_CD_00_exadcel01',
'o/10.0.0.3/DATA_EXAD_CD_01_exadcel01',
'o/10.0.0.3/DATA_EXAD_CD_02_exadcel01',
'o/10.0.0.3/DATA_EXAD_CD_03_exadcel01',
'o/10.0.0.3/DATA_EXAD_CD_04_exadcel01',
'o/10.0.0.3/DATA_EXAD_CD_05_exadcel01',
'o/10.0.0.3/DATA_EXAD_CD_06_exadcel01',
'o/10.0.0.3/DATA_EXAD_CD_07_exadcel01',
'o/10.0.0.3/DATA_EXAD_CD_08_exadcel01',
'o/10.0.0.3/DATA_EXAD_CD_09_exadcel01',
'o/10.0.0.3/DATA_EXAD_CD_10_exadcel01',
'o/10.0.0.3/DATA_EXAD_CD_11_exadcel01'
FAILGROUP EXADCEL02 DISK
'o/10.0.0.4/DATA_EXAD_CD_00_exadcel02',
'o/10.0.0.4/DATA_EXAD_CD_01_exadcel02',
'o/10.0.0.4/DATA_EXAD_CD_02_exadcel02',
'o/10.0.0.4/DATA_EXAD_CD_03_exadcel02',
'o/10.0.0.4/DATA_EXAD_CD_04_exadcel02',
'o/10.0.0.4/DATA_EXAD_CD_05_exadcel02',
'o/10.0.0.4/DATA_EXAD_CD_06_exadcel02',
'o/10.0.0.4/DATA_EXAD_CD_07_exadcel02',
'o/10.0.0.4/DATA_EXAD_CD_08_exadcel02',
'o/10.0.0.4/DATA_EXAD_CD_09_exadcel02',
'o/10.0.0.4/DATA_EXAD_CD_10_exadcel02',
'o/10.0.0.4/DATA_EXAD_CD_11_exadcel02'
```

```
FAILGROUP EXADCEL03 DISK
'o/10.0.0.5/DATA_EXAD_CD_00_exadcel03',
'o/10.0.0.5/DATA_EXAD_CD_01_exadcel03',
'o/10.0.0.5/DATA_EXAD_CD_02_exadcel03',
'o/10.0.0.5/DATA_EXAD_CD_03_exadcel03',
'o/10.0.0.5/DATA_EXAD_CD_04_exadcel03',
'o/10.0.0.5/DATA_EXAD_CD_05_exadcel03',
'o/10.0.0.5/DATA_EXAD_CD_06_exadcel03',
'o/10.0.0.5/DATA_EXAD_CD_07_exadcel03',
'o/10.0.0.5/DATA_EXAD_CD_08_exadcel03',
'o/10.0.0.5/DATA_EXAD_CD_09_exadcel03',
'o/10.0.0.5/DATA_EXAD_CD_10_exadcel03',
'o/10.0.0.5/DATA_EXAD_CD_11_exadcel03'
ATTRIBUTE
  'compatible.asm'='11.2.0.4',
  'compatible.rdbms'='11.2.0.4',
  'au_size'='4M',
  'cell.smart_scan_capable'='TRUE';
```

Configuring ASM Instance with asmca (Singe Instance)

We would use this approach to cloning a non-RAC ASM environment from one server to another. The following code example creates and configures the ASM instance and also creates the DATA disk group.

```
/u01/app/oracle/product/11.2.0/grid/bin/asmca -silent -configureASM \
  -sysAsmPassword oralasm \
  -asmsnmpPassword oralasm \
  -diskstring 'ORCL:*' \
  -diskGroupName 'DATA' \
  -diskList 'ORCL:DATA1','ORCL:DATA2' \
  -au_size 4 \
  -compatible.asm 11.2.0.0 \
  -compatible.rdbms 11.2.0.0 \
  -redundancy external;

ASM created and started successfully.

DiskGroup DATA created successfully.
```

Creating Diskgroup with asmca command line

We always promote command line options over graphical user interfaces because it allows us to automate installs and builds and deliver consistent configurations that are reliable and expedient. We will show examples of how to create disk groups with asmca but with a command line interface (-silent mode).

Here's all the disks that's available for us. OCRVOTE1 disk was consumed when we installed Oracle 12c Release 1 Grid Infrastructure.

```
$ /usr/sbin/oracleasm listdisks
DATA1
DATA2
DATA3
DATA4
FRA1
OCRVOTE1
```

In the simple shell script below, We will create two additional disk groups: DATA and FRA. We will create the DATA disk group first and then proceed with the FRA disk group. For the FRA disk group, we will add one additional compatible.advm property so that we can create an ACFS file system.

```
$ cat asmca_cr_dg.sh
asmca -silent -createDiskGroup \
  -diskGroupName DATA \
  -diskList 'ORCL:DATA1,ORCL:DATA2,ORCL:DATA3,ORCL:DATA4' \
  -redundancy external \
  -au_size 4 -compatible.asm 12.1 \
  -compatible.rdbms 12.1 \
  -sysAsmPassword oracle123

asmca -silent -createDiskGroup \
  -diskGroupName FRA \
  -diskList 'ORCL:FRA1' \
  -redundancy external \
  -au_size 4 -compatible.asm 12.1 \
  -compatible.rdbms 12.1 \
  -compatible.advm 12.1 \
  -sysAsmPassword oracle123

$ ./asmca_cr_dg.sh

Disk Group DATA created successfully.

Disk Group FRA created successfully.
```

Here's a simple command to determine the status of ASM disk groups.

The -A option will tell the grep executable to print 2 additional lines below the matching lines:

```
$ crsctl stat res -t |grep -A 2 ".dg"
ora.DATA.dg
               ONLINE   ONLINE          o159a                    STABLE
               ONLINE   ONLINE          o159b                    STABLE
ora.FRA.dg
               ONLINE   ONLINE          o159a                    STABLE
               ONLINE   ONLINE          o159b                    STABLE
--
ora.OCRVOTE.dg
               ONLINE   ONLINE          o159a                    STABLE
               ONLINE   ONLINE          o159b                    STABLE
```

Rotating ASM Alertlogs (Purge and Archive)

We all have a need to purge our archive logs from the ASM instance. Instead of removing the archivelogs, we will keep the older copies up to X amount of copies as specified in the configuration file and compress the older copies of the archivelogs.

```
$ cat rotate_asm.ksh
export SH=/u01/app/general/sh
export CONF=$SH/asm1.conf
cat <<!! >$CONF
/u01/app/oracle/diag/asm/+asm/+ASM1/trace/alert_+ASM1.log {
weekly
copytruncate
rotate 4
compress
}
!!

logrotate -s $SH/log_rotate_asm1 -f $CONF-s $SH/log_rotate_listener_scan1 -f
$CONF
```

The –s option specifies alternative state file for the logrotate utility. In order for oracle or grid unix account to execute logrotate, the –s option must be specified since the default state file is /var/lib/logrotate.status.

Typically, only the root account has access to write to this file. The –f option specifies the force option to rotate the file with vengenance even if the logrotate utility does not think that the rotate is necessary. The last option to the log rotate is to specifiy the configuration file where we can specify:

- location of the log file to rotate and options to
- frequency of rotation
- number of files to keep
- to compress or not compress

Transferring Backups / Files to Another Data Center

We run into situations where we do not have enough file system space to copy backups or archivelogs from one server to another. For customers on Exadata, they have to either setup DBFS or leverage NFS storage to stage the files. Why go through another storage layer when we can copy files from ASM instance to another ASM instance. Here's a comprehensive script to transfer backups from ASM from the Primary Data Center to the Disaster Recovery Data Center:

```
cat dg_asm_cp.prod1-vip.ksh
# -- Works with Oracle 11.2

export ORACLE_SID=+ASM1
export ORAENV_ASK=NO
. oraenv
unset ORAENV_ASK

echo "supersecret"| asmcmd cp -ifr
+FRADG_S1/dbatools/backupset/2010_08_11/annnf0_TAG20100811T161630_0
.813.726768993 sys@DRPROD-
vip.1521.+ASM1:+FRADG/dbatools/backupset/2010_08_11/annnf0_TAG20100
811T161630_0

echo "supersecret"| asmcmd cp -ifr
+FRADG_S1/dbatools/backupset/2010_08_11/annnf0_TAG20100811T161630_0
.814.726768995 sys@DRPROD-
vip.1521.+ASM1:+FRADG/dbatools/backupset/20

10_08_11/annnf0_TAG20100811T161630_0
echo "supersecret"| asmcmd cp -ifr
```

```
+FRADG_S1/dbatools/backupset/2010_08_11/annnf0_TAG20100811T161630_0
.815.726768995 sys@DRPROD-
vip.1521.+ASM1:+FRADG/dbatools/backupset/2010_08_11/annnf0_TAG20100
811T161630_0

echo "supersecret"| asmcmd cp -ifr
+FRADG_S1/dbatools/backupset/2010_08_11/annnf0_TAG20100811T161630_0
.816.726768999 sys@DRPROD-
vip.1521.+ASM1:+FRADG/dbatools/backupset/2010_08_11/annnf0_TAG20100
811T161630_0

echo "supersecret"| asmcmd cp -ifr
+FRADG_S1/dbatools/backupset/2010_08_11/annnf0_TAG20100811T161630_0
.817.726769001 sys@DRPROD-
vip.1521.+ASM1:+FRADG/dbatools/backupset/2010_08_11/annnf0_TAG20100
811T161630_0

echo "supersecret"| asmcmd cp -ifr
+FRADG_S1/dbatools/backupset/2010_08_11/ncnnf0_DBATOOLS1_CTL_11AUG1
0_1615_0.818.726769005 sys@DRPROD-
vip.1521.+ASM1:+FRADG/dbatools/backupset/2010_08_11/ncnnf0_DBATOOLS
1_CTL_11AUG10_1615_0
...
```

Leveraging Calibrate I/O to Determine Potential IOPs

For an existing database you can calculate IOP and throughput capabilities with oracle's built-in Calibrate IO which is a built in component of the DBMS Resource Manager. The Calibrate IO feature of Oracle Database is accessed using the DBMS_RESOURCE_MANAGER.CALIBRATE_IO procedure. The CALIBRATE_IO procedure performs I/O intensive read-only workload composed of one megabytes of random of I/Os to the existing database files to determine the maximum IOPS (I/O requests per second) and MBPS (megabytes of I/O per second) that can be sustained by the storage subsystem. The CALIBRATE_IO procedure is induces significant performance workload and should only be executed when the database is relatively idle (i.e. late nights or weekends when database workload will not impact other database tasks).

```
set serveroutput on size unlimited
set time on timing on echo on
set serveroutput on size unlimited
set time on timing on echo on

declare
max_iops integer;
max_mbps integer;
actual_latency integer;
begin
dbms_resource_manager.calibrate_io (
num_physical_disks => 48,
max_latency => 10,
max_iops => max_iops,
max_mbps => max_mbps,
actual_latency => actual_latency);
dbms_output.put_line ('Max IOPS = '|| max_iops);
dbms_output.put_line ('Max MBPS = '|| max_mbps);
dbms_output.put_line ('Latency = '|| actual_latency);
end;
/

Max IOPS = 80075
Max MBPS = 1484
Latency = 2
```

Here's some notes for you to think about:

- num_physical_disks is not the number of LUNs. It is the number of disks the LUNs are comprised of.
- The default max_latency is set to 20 milliseconds if you do not provide a value for this parameter. This parameter defines the maximum tolerable latency for database I/O requests. We should set this to a value of 10
- The output for this stored procedure will be max IOPs (maximum number of randomly distributed I/O requests per second that can be sustained) and MBPS (maximum throughput for I/O that can be sustained)
- The calibration result is available from the V$IO_CALIBRATION_STATUS view. Successful calibration results are located in DBA_RSRC_IO_CALIBRATE table.
- Only one calibration can be executed at the same time, and you

need SYSDBA privileges to execute this stored procedure.

You can leverage the print_table from TomKyte's website:

```
SQL> exec print_table(' select inst_id, status, calibration_time from
gv$io_calibration_status');
INST_ID : 1
STATUS : IN PROGRESS
CALIBRATION_TIME :
```

Eventually, the status from change to a READY state. Now, you can query the DBA_RSRC_IO_CALIBRATE view:

```
SQL> exec print_table('select * from dba_rsrc_io_calibrate');
```

Benchmarking Storage Performance with Orion

Storage I/O Calibration and benchmarking is a critical component for heavy Oracle database workloads. Lot of companies do not do any kind of I/O benchmarking before or after the implementation. We would like to challenge you to perform benchmarking prior to installing any Oracle software. The objective of the benchmarking is to identify IOP capabilities and throughput for the storage presented to the database servers while identifying latency. We can proactive identify storage, HBA, disk layout, or multi-pathing issues, before laying down any Oracle software. The goal of the benchmarking is to produce a report that will display read and write capabilities of the storage.

Storage benchmarking is a simple process. At a minimum, we recommend running two sets of tests, a maximum throughput sequential write test and a maximum throughput sequential read test. There are many open source tools available to perform those tests. I/O benchmarking is a relatively simple process. Your benchmark criteria needs to include read/write ratios. We need to estimate the % of write activity relative to % of read activity for the presumed workload. Based on the % of writes to read and the RAID implementation, we will be able to decipher the output from the various tools listed below:

1   Oracle Orion (comes shipped starting with Oracle Database 11g
        Release 2)
2   SLOB / SLOB2 - The Silly Little Oracle Benchmark
3   Hammerora – open source oracle load test tool
4   IOzone
5   Linux/Unix dd
6   Swingbench
7   IOmeter

Two of the most popular IO Calibration tools for Oracle environments are Oracle Orion and Swingbench. SLOB and SLOB2 are getting more and more popular among the EMC storage folks. In this section, we will only concentrate on Orion (Upcoming updates to this chapter will incorporate SLOB2 and Swingbench).

We will provide 2 simplified example executions of Orion: one which only simulates reads and the other which will simulate 25% writes and reads. Here's the first example of the Orion execution with 100% reads:

```
ORION VERSION 11.2.0.3.0

Command line:
-run advanced -testname VNA -size_small 32 -size_large 512 -type rand -matrix
basic

These options enable these settings:
Test: mcafee
Small IO size: 32 KB
Large IO size: 512 KB
IO types: small random IOs, large random IOs
Sequential stream pattern: one LUN per stream
Writes: 0%
Cache size: not specified
Duration for each data point: 60 seconds
Small Columns:,      0
Large
Columns:,      0,      1,      2,      3,      6,      9,      12,      15,
    18,     21,     24,     27,     30,     33,     36,     39
Total Data Points: 40

Maximum Large MBPS=797.26 @ Small=0 and Large=39

Maximum Small IOPS=22672 @ Small=95 and Large=0
```

```
Small Read Latency: avg=4189 us, min=584 us, max=75700 us, std dev=2501 us @
Small=95 and Large=0

Minimum Small Latency=304.26 usecs @ Small=1 and Large=0
Small Read Latency: avg=304 us, min=158 us, max=50216 us, std dev=848 us @
Small=1 and Large=0
```

This second execution of Orion simulates 25% writes which is more indicative of a mixed database workload scenario.

```
-run advanced -testname VNA -write 25 -matrix basic

These options enable these settings:
Test: mcafee
Small IO size: 8 KB
Large IO size: 1024 KB
IO types: small random IOs, large random IOs
Sequential stream pattern: one LUN per stream
Writes: 25%
Cache size: not specified
Duration for each data point: 60 seconds

Maximum Large MBPS=732.15 @ Small=0 and Large=27

Maximum Small IOPS=16160 @ Small=45 and Large=0
Small Read Latency: avg=2811 us, min=143 us, max=78562 us, std dev=3168 us @
Small=45 and Large=0
Small Write Latency: avg=2700 us, min=319 us, max=61802 us, std dev=1589 us @
Small=45 and Large=0

Minimum Small Latency=325.37 usecs @ Small=2 and Large=0
Small Read Latency: avg=242 us, min=115 us, max=60863 us, std dev=806 us @
Small=2 and Large=0
Small Write Latency: avg=574 us, min=240 us, max=28580 us, std dev=423 us @
Small=2 and Large=0
```

As you can see, as you induce writes, the IOP performance degrades significantly. It is extremely important that you know the workload characteristic of the database that you are about to virtualize. In our simple example, we see IOP performance degrade from 22.6k to 16.1k by simulating 25% writes. Also, your choices in RAID will also determine your IOP performance impact for writes. RAID 5 performance degradation for writes will increase significantly more than with the RAID 10 options. For more advanced Orion testing, you can choose other options such as cache_size and duration.

```
sudo -u root ./orion_linux_x86-64 -run advanced -testname VNA -num_disks 20 -
cache_size 8000 -duration 240 -matrix basic
```

For RAC configurations, you need to execute Orion on all the RAC nodes at the same time. Your output numbers of latency may be impacted. If you have an existing database on a server, you can only leverage Orion in 100% read only mode (which is default). Performing read-only execution of Orion will scare lot of managers as Orion is known to be destructive.

Determining ASM Diskgroup and Disk Free Information from the OS Shell Script

```
export DB=$(ps -ef |grep +ASM |grep -i pmon |awk {'print $8'} |sed -e
's/asm_pmon_//g')

export ORACLE_SID=${DB}
export ORAENV_ASK=NO
. oraenv

sqlplus -s / as sysasm <<!!
col name for a15
col path for a20
set lines 122 pages 66
col AU for 9 hea 'AU|MB'
col state for a12
col compatibility for a10 hea 'ASM|Compat'
col database_compatibility for a10 hea 'Database|Compat'
col pct_Free for 99.99 head 'Pct|Free'
col block_size for 99,999 head 'Block|Size'
col Total_GB for 999,999.99 head 'Total|GB'
col Free_GB for 999,999.99 head 'Free|GB'

col pct_free for 999 hea 'Pct|Free'
select name, path,
       total_mb,
       free_mb,
       round(free_mb/total_mb*100,2) pct_Free
from v\$asm_disk
where total_mb >1
order by name;

select name, state,
```

```
        round(total_mb/1024,2) Total_GB,
        round(free_mb/1024,2) Free_GB,
        round(free_mb/total_mb*100,2) pct_Free,
        allocation_unit_size/1024/1024 AU,
        compatibility,
        database_compatibility
from v\$asm_diskgroup
where total_mb > 1;
!!
```

Here's sample output from the code example:

NAME	PATH	TOTAL_MB	FREE_MB	Pct Free
DATA1	ORCL:DATA1	12800	8372	65
DATA2	ORCL:DATA2	51196	33612	66
OCR1	ORCL:OCR1	12799	9160	72
OCR2	ORCL:OCR2	12800	9150	71
OCR3	ORCL:OCR3	12800	9154	72
RECO1	ORCL:RECO1	51196	40516	79

6 rows selected.

NAME	STATE	Total GB	Free GB	Pct Free	AU MB	ASM Compat	Database Compat
RECO	MOUNTED	50.00	39.57	79	4	12.1.0.0.0	10.1.0.0.0
OCR	MOUNTED	37.50	26.82	72	1	12.1.0.0.0	10.1.0.0.0
DATA	MOUNTED	62.50	41.00	66	4	12.1.0.0.0	10.1.0.0.0

We can modify this script to filter on PCT_FREE on 10% to 20% and send alerts when the disk groups are about to run out of free space. Or DBAs can send output of this script to their email addresses every day as part of the ASM space utilization report. The best use case for this script has been to send critical alerts when the disk group space threshold creeps beyond the 10% of free space.

Moving the Vote Disk (on Exadata in this example)

```
+ASM1 - root: crsctl query css votedisk
##  STATE    File Universal Id                File Name Disk group
--  -----    ------------------               --------- ---------
 1. ONLINE   8985c1d4c2154fa8bfdb037c8c86b9e0
(o/192.168.10.10/DATA_EXAP_CD_00_exapcel06) [DATA_EXAP]
 2. ONLINE   9d4da85d535d4fb9bfe6973f865b6d39
(o/192.168.10.11/DATA_EXAP_CD_00_exapcel07) [DATA_EXAP]
```

```
 3. ONLINE    9fb080f7cd704fadbf500c986272ef45
(o/192.168.10.5/DATA_EXAP_CD_00_exapce101) [DATA_EXAP]
 4. ONLINE    b1c5e1cdc83e4fd9bf8f05b726ed2f98
(o/192.168.10.7/DATA_EXAP_CD_00_exapce103) [DATA_EXAP]
 5. ONLINE    0e3423d2a77d4f72bf3a25fcc268485b
(o/192.168.10.8/DATA_EXAP_CD_00_exapce104) [DATA_EXAP]
Located 5 voting disk(s).

+ASM1 - root: crsctl replace votedisk +DBFS_DG
Successful addition of voting disk 6df3a8120a3d4f24bf56850f5ea09694.
Successful addition of voting disk 72129b8b34994f0fbff9fc7b7abab58c.
Successful addition of voting disk a77bf05177d84f06bf082e9110761e15.
Successful deletion of voting disk 8985c1d4c2154fa8bfdb037c8c86b9e0.
Successful deletion of voting disk 9d4da85d535d4fb9bfe6973f865b6d39.
Successful deletion of voting disk 9fb080f7cd704fadbf500c986272ef45.
Successful deletion of voting disk b1c5e1cdc83e4fd9bf8f05b726ed2f98.
Successful deletion of voting disk 0e3423d2a77d4f72bf3a25fcc268485b.
Successfully replaced voting disk group with +DBFS_DG.
CRS-4266: Voting file(s) successfully replaced
```

Check Vote Disks after the move:

```
$ crsctl query css votedisk
##  STATE    File Universal Id                   File Name Disk group
--  -----    -----------------                   --------- ----------
 1. ONLINE   6df3a8120a3d4f24bf56850f5ea09694
(o/192.168.10.5/DBFS_DG_CD_02_exapce101) [DBFS_DG]
 2. ONLINE   72129b8b34994f0fbff9fc7b7abab58c
(o/192.168.10.6/DBFS_DG_CD_02_exapce102) [DBFS_DG]
 3. ONLINE   a77bf05177d84f06bf082e9110761e15
(o/192.168.10.7/DBFS_DG_CD_02_exapce103) [DBFS_DG]
```

Moving the OCR Disk (on Exadata in this example)

First check current OCR information

```
+ASM1 - root: ocrcheck
Status of Oracle Cluster Registry is as follows :
         Version                  :          3
         Total space (kbytes)     :     262120
         Used space (kbytes)      :       3196
         Available space (kbytes) :     258924
         ID                       :  386215515
         Device/File Name         : +DATA_EXAP
                                    Device/File integrity check succeeded

                                    Device/File not configured

                                    Device/File not configured
```

```
                            Device/File not configured

                            Device/File not configured

        Cluster registry integrity check succeeded

        Logical corruption check succeeded
```

Add OCR to new DiskGroup Location:

```
+ASM1 - root: ocrconfig -add +DBFS_DG
```

Perform Check of OCR Locations Again. Notice the two locations:

```
+ASM1 - root: ocrcheck
Status of Oracle Cluster Registry is as follows :
        Version                   :        3
        Total space (kbytes)      :    262120
        Used space (kbytes)       :      3196
        Available space (kbytes)  :    258924
        ID                        :  386215515
        Device/File Name          : +DATA_EXAP
                            Device/File integrity check succeeded
        Device/File Name          :   +DBFS_DG
                            Device/File integrity check succeeded

                            Device/File not configured

                            Device/File not configured

                            Device/File not configured

        Cluster registry integrity check succeeded

        Logical corruption check succeeded
```

Delete the OLD OCR Location

```
+ASM1 - root: ocrconfig -delete +DATA_EXAP
exapdb01:/tmp/dba
```

Perform OCR Check again:

```
+ASM1 - root: ocrcheck
Status of Oracle Cluster Registry is as follows :
        Version                   :        3
        Total space (kbytes)      :    262120
        Used space (kbytes)       :      3196
        Available space (kbytes)  :    258924
        ID                        :  386215515
        Device/File Name          :   +DBFS_DG
                            Device/File integrity check succeeded
```

```
                                   Device/File not configured

                                   Device/File not configured

                                   Device/File not configured

                                   Device/File not configured

            Cluster registry integrity check succeeded
```

Run cluvfy and check on OCR

```
$ cluvfy comp ocr

Verifying OCR integrity

Checking OCR integrity...

Checking the absence of a non-clustered configuration...
All nodes free of non-clustered, local-only configurations


ASM Running check passed. ASM is running on all specified nodes

Checking OCR config file "/etc/oracle/ocr.loc"...

OCR config file "/etc/oracle/ocr.loc" check successful


Disk group for ocr location "+DBFS_DG" available on all the nodes


NOTE:
This check does not verify the integrity of the OCR contents. Execute
'ocrcheck' as a privileged user to verify the contents of OCR.

OCR integrity check passed

Verification of OCR integrity was successful.
```

Migrating to ASM from the File System Leveraging RMAN

Couple of options is available to migrate Oracle databases from the file system to ASM. One method is to leverage RMAN, and another method method is to leverage the asmcmd cp command.

RMAN Image Copy to ASM

We will focus on the RMAN approach with the RMAN image copies.

```
RMAN> run
2> {
3> allocate channel d1 type disk format '+data';
4> backup as copy database;
5> release channel d1;
6> }
allocated channel: d1
channel d1: SID=154 device type=DISK

Starting backup at 12-MAY-08
channel d1: starting datafile copy
input datafile file number=00001 name=/data/oracle/DBATOOLS/system01.dbf
output file name=+DATA/dbatools/datafile/system.256.654520605
tag=TAG20080512T111635 RECID=2 STAMP=654520833
channel d1: datafile copy complete, elapsed time: 00:03:56
channel d1: starting datafile copy
[...]
input datafile file number=00004 name=/data/oracle/DBATOOLS/users01.dbf
output file name=+DATA/dbatools/datafile/users.261.654521041
tag=TAG20080512T111635 RECID=7 STAMP=654521042
channel d1: datafile copy complete, elapsed time: 00:00:01
Finished backup at 12-MAY-08

released channel: d1

RMAN>
RMAN> **end-of-file**
```

If you have multi-terabyte databases, you will want to allocate many channels. Allocating 16 channels for this is not unheard of to drive throughput on the RMAN image copy. You should be able to drive multiple terabytes of transfers per hour depending on storage that you have. At a minimum, you should be able to drive 1TB per hour even on the older storage arrays.

Update Controlfile

Once the backup is complete, we need to update the controlfile to point to the new location of the datafiles. To update the controlfile, we can use the RMAN switch command:

```
RMAN> switch database to copy;
datafile 1 switched to datafile copy
"+DATA/dbatools/datafile/system.256.654520605"
[..]
datafile 5 switched to datafile copy
"+DATA/dbatools/datafile/example.258.654521005"
```

After we switch our database to the image copy, we will need to apply archive logs necessary to bring the database in ASM in 100% synchronization with the database on the file system. Once the last of the archivelogs are applied, we will open resetlog the database inside of ASM.

Move Controlfile to ASM

We still have controlfiles, temporary tablspaces, and redo logs that need to be migrated to ASM. Again, we have couple of approaches to migrate the control file to ASM. We can rebuild the controlfile from trace with the "alter database backup controlfile to trace" command. Or we can shutdown the database and nomount the database restore the controlfile using RMAN restore command. Let's assume that we have shutdown the database and placed the database in nomount mode. We will issue the RMAN restore command twice. We will restore the controlfile to the +DATA disk group and restore another copy of the controlfile to the +FRA disk group.

```
RMAN> restore controlfile to '+data' from
'/data/oracle/DBATOOLS/control01.ctl';
```

```
RMAN> restore controlfile to '+fra' from
'/data/oracle/DBATOOLS/control01.ctl';
Starting restore at 12-MAY-08
using channel ORA_DISK_1

channel ORA_DISK_1: copied control file copy
Finished restore at 12-MAY-08
```

As we restore the controlfiles to the two disk groups, we are adhering to the best practices and creating a mirror copy of our controlfiles. Next, let's locate our controlfiles and update our initialization parameter for ASM:

```
ASMCMD> pwd
+data/DBATOOLS

ASMCMD> find --type controlfile +data/DBATOOLS *
+data/DBATOOLS/CONTROLFILE/Backup.326.856868859
+data/DBATOOLS/CONTROLFILE/current.328.856869255
```

Note: The --type option specifies the type of file.

Repeat the find command for the +FRA diskgroup.   Once we locate both of the control files, we can issue the alter system command to update our SPFILE:

```
SQL> alter system set
control_files='+data/DBATOOLS/CONTROLFILE/current.328.856869255','+FRA/DBATOO
LS/CONTROLFILE/current.299.654527065' scope=spfile;
```

After we update the respective changes to the SPFILE, we must bounce the database instance for the changes to be reflected. After we re-start the database, we can proceed to move the temporary tablespaces to ASM.

Move Temp Tablespaces to ASM

The steps to move the temp tablespace is relatively straight forward and involves the following steps:

- set the new database default to the staging temp directory (temp2)
- drop the original temp tablespace (temp)
- create the original temp tablespace in ASM (temp)
- set the new database default to temp
- drop the staging's temp tablespace

Here's a simple code example to move your temp tablespace files from the file system to ASM:

```
create temporary tablespace temp2 tempfile '+data' size 4g autoextend on;
alter database default temporary tablespace temp2;
drop tablespace temp;
create temporary tablespace temp tempfile '+data' size 4g autoextend on;
alter database default temporary tablespace temp;
drop tablespace temp2;
```

Move Redo to ASM

We are almost done with moving the database to ASM. The last thing that we must do is move the redo logs to ASM.

```
  1* alter database add logfile group 10 ('+data', '+fra') size 100m
SQL> /

Database altered.
```

We need to repeat the same steps for Group number 11,12, and 13. You can call the group numbers whatever you want but we like to create a group number to reflect the instance number. Once we created new set of redo logs inside of ASM, we need to delete all the members from the OS file system.

```
  1* select group#, member from v$logfile
SQL> /

    GROUP# MEMBER
```

```
----------  ----------------------------------------------------------
   4 /data/oracle/DBATOOLS/redo04.log
   3 /data/oracle/DBATOOLS/redo03.log
   2 /data/oracle/DBATOOLS/redo02.log
   1 /data/oracle/DBATOOLS/redo01.log
  10 +DATA/dbatools/onlinelog/group_10.262.654528555
  10 +FRA/dbatools/onlinelog/group_10.257.654528555
  11 +DATA/dbatools/onlinelog/group_11.264.654528583
  11 +FRA/dbatools/onlinelog/group_11.258.654528583
  12 +DATA/dbatools/onlinelog/group_12.263.654528599
  12 +FRA/dbatools/onlinelog/group_12.259.654528599
  13 +DATA/dbatools/onlinelog/group_13.266.654528613
  13 +FRA/dbatools/onlinelog/group_13.260.654528623

12 rows selected.
```

We have identified all the redo logs. Let's switch through all the redo logs and remove the redo logs that are no longer active.

```
alter system archive log current;
alter system switch logfile;


SQL> alter database drop logfile group 1;

Database altered.
```

We need to repeat the "alter system drop logfile group" command for for group number 2,3,4. One we have successfully moved the redo logs to ASM, our job is done.

Reducing Our Downtime to Migrate to ASM Using Forever Incremental Updates

Earlier we learned how to move a database from file system to ASM. What do you do when the database in 10's or 100's of terabytes or even in the petabyte range. We will have to take an enormous amount of downtime to move the database from the file system to ASM. With the RMAN Forever Incremental Updates approach, we can reduce that outage window to 15-30 minutes (or even less) depending on how much you have scripted

Here's the fundamental concept. We perform a RMAN image copy backup from the file system to the ASM +data disk group. We take incremental backups and we apply the incremental backups to the +data disk group. We repeat the incremental backups and apply (referred to as Forever Incremental Updates) as much as we need to keep the image copy in sync with the on-line transactional database that is running on the file system. We incur a small outage window during the weekend, perform our final incremental update, switch the database from the file system to the database copy on ASM, and apply any archivelog to bring the database to complete consistency.

We have scripted the entire process to move the database to ASM (or even move the database back to file system) based on the configuration file. We specified a parameter called BKUP_DIR. Depending on wether you specify this location to be an ASM disk group or a file system directory, the backup and incremental update will occur to this location.

```
$ cat rman.conf
BKUP_DIR=/tmp/dba/${ORACLE_SID}
IMAGE_COPY_DIR=+DATA

# --
# --
RMAN_IMAGE=rman_${ORACLE_SID}.image.rcv
RMAN_INC=rman_${ORACLE_SID}.incremental.rcv
RMAN_FINAL=rman_${ORACLE_SID}.final.rcv
RMAN_UPDATE=rman_update
```

Note:
We have also created 5 additional parameters in the rman.conf configuration file that will be leveraged in our RMAN script called rman.image.ksh. The BKUP_DIR and IMAGE_COPY_DIR is dynamically substituted in the rman.image.ksh script in the shell script with sed:

```
$ cat rman.image
run
{
allocate channel d1 type disk;
```

```
allocate channel d2 type disk;
allocate channel d3 type disk;
allocate channel d4 type disk;
backup as copy incremental level 0 tag=MIG format '###_IMAGE_COPY_DIR_###/%U'
(database) ;
release channel d1;
release channel d2;
release channel d3;
release channel d4;
}
```

The rman.image.ksh script invokes the rman.image script but before it does, it replaces the ###_IMAGE_COPY_DIR_### and ###_BKUP_DIR_### with what is in rman.conf. In this example, the baseline image copy of the database is tagged with the keywords 'MIG'. You will notice in all the RMAN scripts, RMAN tags play a very important role.

```
$ cat rman.image.ksh
. $PWD/rman.conf

touch ${BKUP_DIR}/rman.testfile
[ $? -ne 0 ] && { echo "Cannot write to $BKUP_DIR ... Exiting!!\n"; exit 1; }

export NLS_DATE_FORMAT='DD-MON-RR HH24:MI:SS'
cat rman.image |sed -e "s.###_IMAGE_COPY_DIR_###.$IMAGE_COPY_DIR.g" \
               |sed -e "s.###_BKUP_DIR_###.$BKUP_DIR.g" \
                  > ${RMAN_IMAGE}
#rman target / cmdfile ${RMAN_IMAGE} log ${RMAN_IMAGE}.log
```

Perform RMAN Incremental Backup

Next we can execute the rman.update.ksh script. The rman.update.ksh script performs the incremental backup ready to be applied against the image copy backup. Here's the contents of the rman.update.ksh script:

```
cat rman.update.ksh
. $PWD/rman.conf

touch ${BKUP_DIR}/rman.testfile
[ $? -ne 0 ] && { echo "Cannot write to $BKUP_DIR ...
Exiting!!\n"; exit 1; }

export NLS_DATE_FORMAT='DD-MON-RR HH24:MI:SS'
```

```
cat  rman.inc  |sed  -e  "s.###_BKUP_DIR_###.$BKUP_DIR.g"  >
${RMAN_INC}
#rman target / cmdfile ${RMAN_INC}
#rman target / cmdfile ${RMAN_UPDATE}
```

The rman.update.ksh shell script can automatically invoke the rman.inc script. You can choose to run the incremental back manually or have the rman.update.ksh script do it for you.

```
cat rman.inc
run
{
allocate channel d1 type disk;
allocate channel d2 type disk;
BACKUP INCREMENTAL LEVEL 1 tag='INC' FOR RECOVER OF COPY WITH TAG 'MIG'
format '###_BKUP_DIR_###/%d.%s.%p.%t.L1.4R.DB' DATABASE;

sql "alter system archive log current";
sql "alter system switch logfile";
sql "alter system switch logfile";
backup format '###_BKUP_DIR_###/%d.%s.%p.%t.A' skip inaccessible archivelog
all not backed up;

release channel d1;
release channel d2;
}
```

Again, the incremental backup will write to the BKUP_DIR that's defined in the rman.conf file.

Perform RMAN Incremental Update

Next, we will update the image copy of the database with our last incremental backup.

```
cat rman.update
run
{
allocate channel d1 type disk;
allocate channel d2 type disk;
recover copy of database with tag 'MIG' from tag 'INC';
release channel d1;
release channel d2;
}
```

The last incremental backup was tagged with the keyword 'INC'. We will need to perform in the section above **Perform RMAN Incremental Backup** and **Perform RMAN Incremental Update** as often as needed to bring the image copy of the database close to be in sync with the production database on the file system.

Perform Final Archive Log and Controlfile Backup

At the time of cutover, we will perform a last and final incremental backup and update (**Perform RMAN Incremental Backup** and **Perform RMAN Incremental Update**) as well as performing a backup of the archivelog and controlfile for the production database. You should do this with the database in a mounted state (Briefly shutdown the source database).

```
cat rman.final
run {
allocate channel d1 type disk;
allocate channel d2 type disk;

sql "alter system archive log current";
sql "alter system switch logfile";
sql "alter system switch logfile";
backup tag='LAST_ARCH_MIG' format '###_BKUP_DIR_###/%d.%s.%p.%t.A' skip
inaccessible archivelog all not backed up;

backup as copy tag=MIGCTL format '###_BKUP_DIR_###/%d.%s.%p.%t.CTL' (current
controlfile);
backup spfile format '###_BKUP_DIR_###/%d.%s.%p.%t.SPFILE';
sql "create pfile=''/tmp/dba/RMANDR/initRMANDR.ora'' from spfile";

release channel d1;
release channel d2;
}
```

After the final backups are complete, we will switch our database to the image copy and apply any archive logs necessary to bring the databases in 100% synchronization. Once the last of the archivelogs are applied, we will open resetlog the database inside of ASM.

Next perform the similar step by step instructions specified in **Move**

Controlfile to ASM, **Move Temp Tablespaces to ASM** and **Move Redo to ASM** from the sections above and all your database files will be inside of ASM.

This section clearly was about reducing the downtime to move the database from the file system to ASM. As we mentioned before, even the largest of the databases can be moved from file system to ASM in less than 15-30 minutes. If your outage window requirements are less than 15-30 minutes, you should consider Data Guard to ASM and performing a switchover process. This approach not only reduces your outage window even more but also give you a contingency plan in the event, you happen to run into performance issues on ASM for some reason (i.e. misconfiguration of storage).

Conclusion

Since its inception, ASM has grown from being a purpose-built volume manager for the database to a feature-rich storage manager that supports all database related files, includes a POSIX-complaint cluster file system, in addition ASM has become the center piece of the Oracle Engineered Systems. 12c ASM addresses extreme scalability, management of real-world data types and remove many of the limitations of previous generations ASM. ASM has evolved with the Cloud Computing demands of consolidation, high utilization and high availability.

Made in the USA
Columbia, SC
11 June 2017